J. Palmer

List of early printed and other Books in the Possession of Dr.

Corrie

J. Palmer

List of early printed and other Books in the Possession of Dr. Corrie

ISBN/EAN: 9783337249946

Printed in Europe, USA, Canada, Australia, Japan

Cover: Foto ©Andreas Hilbeck / pixelio.de

More available books at **www.hansebooks.com**

LIST

OF

Printed and other Books

IN THE POSSESSION OF

DR. CORRIE

MASTER OF JESUS COLLEGE, CAMBRIDGE.

———————

Cambridge:
PRINTED BY J. PALMER.
1880.

EARLY PRINTED BOOKS

IN THE LIBRARY OF

THE MASTER OF JESUS COLLEGE, CAMBRIDGE.

1

SERMONES XXXII Aurei Venerabilis Domini Alberti Magni Episcopi Ratisponensis, de sacrosancto Eucharistiæ Sacramento. The colophon: Coloniæ impensis Henrici Quentell impressi Anno Sancti Domini MCCCCXCVIII. [Hain, 454]

This book is small 4to, and is of a rare edition. The first edition of these Sermons appeared in 8vo, soon after the invention of printing; the second in folio, in 1474 at Cologne, without name, place or date; the third edition in Mayence, in folio, printed by John Guldenschaff. This fourth edition is rare (see Clement, *Bibliotheque Curieuse*, Vol. 1, p. 123 et seq.) and is not mentioned by Brunet nor Ebert. A fine clean copy. On the title-page is a wood engraving representing the Infant Christ with the heavenly Dove hovering, the Virgin, with Joseph, Zacharias and Elizabeth in attendance.

1a

SERMONES XXXII Aurei Venerabilis Domini Alberti Magni Episcopi Ratisponensis, de sacrosancto Eucharistiæ Sacramento. The colophon: Expliciunt Sermones de Sacramento Corporis et Sanguinis Domini, a Venerabili Doctore Alberto magno editi accuratissima quoque correctione cura insertione Sermonis xxii (qui a prius impressis defecerat). Coloniæ impensis Henrici Quentell impressi Anno Sancti Domini MCCCCXCVIII. [Hain, 454]

On the title-page is a woodcut representing our Lord as an infant seated on an altar, held by one hand by the Virgin, Elizabeth holding the other, attended by Joseph on one side and by Zachariah on the other, who holds a paten and chalice. Overhead is a representation of the Holy Spirit in the form of a dove surrounded with a nimbus. At the foot of the altar is a shield bearing three crowns in chief.

2
VITÆ PATRUM. (On a fly leaf, in a fine bold letter).
The colophon: Deo gratias. In alma Venetiarum urbe man-
dato impensisque probatissimi viri Domini Nicholai de
Franckfordia Anno Domini MCCCCCXII die XX Septembris.

This book is the Legendary of Jacobus de Voragine or Lombardic
history (?), only arranged under four divisions. The first part
forms the history, the second is for instruction and doctrinal
purposes, the third relates to the observance of rules, and the
last has respect to the commendation of the virtues of life.
The border of the first leaf of the History is adorned with wood
engravings, as also are the capital letters throughout the book,
some of the latter representing some action of the Saint to whose
legend it is prefixed. It is paged by Arabic numerals. The book
is a good specimen of the Venetian press, on vellum-paper and
is clean and in good condition. The book begins with a table of
seven leaves of matter contained in the book.

5
D. DIONYSII Carthusiani Epistolarum ac Evangeliorum
Dominicalium totius anni Enarratio, adjunctis Homiliis et
Sermonibus variis tam ad plebem, quam ad religiosos om-
nipharia eruditione conspicuis. Pars prima de Tempore.
Coloniæ P. Quentell suis impensis excudebat, Anno, MDXXXIII.
Cum Gratia et Privilegio.

The title to the second volume is mainly similar to that of the first,
with the words "Pars Altera de Sanctis." The title page of both
is elaborately engraved by Anthony von Worms, a German
engraver of that period.

6
AUREI SERMONES totius anni de tempore et de Sanctis
cum quadragesimali pluribusque extravagantibus Sermonibus
Sacræ pagine eximii Professoris Magistri Johannis Nider
Ordinis Prædicatorum Conventus Nurembergensis. Qui pro-
fecto idcirco aurei nominantur et sunt, Tum propter precio-
sissimam materiam quam tractant, Tum propter efficacissimas
rerum quas tractant probaciones, Tum propter amplissimam
eorundem capacitatem ut vix videatur materia predicabilis

populo quam compendissime non comprehendant ut patet ex registris eorundem sermonum huic libro impressis, Tum propter excellentiam autoris qui quante excellentie fuerit in facultate theologica ejus scripta super sententias aliaque luculentur ostendunt.

The author of this book was a German Dominican Friar, and was commissioned to invite the Bohemians to the Council of Basle. He was the author of several other works. This book is without signatures, name of printer, date or place. The sermons "de tempore" and "de Sanctis" have the word "Sermo" with the Roman numerals as a kind of running title. The book is evidently of an early type of letter. A former owner of the book accordingly refers the printing to Pisandler at Reutlinger in 1482—3. Panzer ii. 404, 49; but Gesner states that the "Sermones de tempore, de Sanctis et Quadragesimali" were printed at the same time at Ulm, by one of the Zainers. The water-mark of the paper is the ox-head used by so many early printers. The book is in old binding, and in good condition, clean and with broad margins.

7

SERMONES DOMINICALES per anni circulum, Magistri Pauli Wan Sacræ paginæ Professoris eximii Ecclesiæque Pataviensis verbi Dei Concionatoris famosissimi. Printed at Hagenau by Henry Gran, 11th Feb., 1517.

This book has two well-executed engraved title pages, and is bound in hog's skin, with brass clasps, and is in excellent condition.

8

SUMMA DE CASIBUS per fratrem Astesanum de ordine fratrum minorum compilata ad honorem Dei immortalis et diligentem exhortationem Domini Johannis Gaietani, Diaconi Cardinalis S. Theodori.

Summe confessionis operi nobilissimo et huic facultati operam dantibus pernecessario quam frater Astesanus de Ast ordinis minorum doctor solemnis edidit maxima cura et sollicitudine famosissimi sacræ theologie magistri fratris Bartholomei de Bellati de Feltro circa juris cottatomes necnon fratris Gomerii Hispani de Ulyxbona provincie Portugalie sacre theologie

bacchalarii clarissimi in conventu Venetiarum circa residuum
totius voluminis ambo ejusdem religionis minorum emendate
sumptibus et jussu Johannis de Colonia sociique ejus Johannis
Manthen de Gherretzem, Venetiis finis impositus est 1478, Die
18. mensis Martii. [Hain, 1893]

The work is divided into eight books, there being prefixed to each
book a list of the cases treated of in it. At the end of the Summa
is a Tabula of the signification of the terms used, appended to
which is a table of the several titles of the Decretals in which the
cases mentioned in the book are treated of. This is a beautiful
copy on vellum-like paper in fine small type in double columns,
fifty-four lines in a column, with clean broad margins. The
initial letters illuminated as far as book vi. chap. 30.

9
DURANDI Rationale divinorum Officiorum (without printer's
name) 1493. Sexta feria ante festum Mariæ Magdalene.
[Hain, 6496]

10
FASCICULUS Temporum (ending in the year 1484). [Hain,
6934]

The title of this Book is on the first leaf, and on the reverse is a
wood-cut representing a person in the act of presenting a book
to his sovereign, who is seated and crowned, holding a sceptre.
The table which follows occupies five leaves: then follow ninety
leaves all regularly numbered. The book is in old binding with
clasps, and some of the leaves are slightly wormed.

12
INSIGNIS duarum passionum Domini Jesu Christi Nostri
Salvatoris Collector quorundam Divini verbi dissertissimorum
prædicatorum doctrinalis et devotionis excitatia (sic) pro die
Veneris sancta sacræ Parasceuen utique vulgo predicabili con-
gruentissima textuáliter ex quatuor Evangeliorum concordantiis,
&c. Simulque continens illibatæ Virginis Sanctæ Katharinæ
passionem seu martyrii ejusdem historiam etc. [Hain, 5480]

This scarce specimen of early printing has signatures but has
neither name of place nor printer, but was printed at Cologne by

John Koelhoff, 1477. (See Panzer i. 337, 453.) The peculiarity
of this book is that both sides of the leaves seem to have been
printed at the same time. I have two copies (one much cleaner
than the other) which are manifestly of the same impression, but
the illuminated capitals are not done in each by the same hand.
[See the word "designt." in last line but one on sig. a2, and
"vinculatus" in last line on same signature.]

14

*SERMONES super Epistolas dominicales per totius Anni
Circulum, collecti ex sermonibus Wilhelmi Parisiensis, et
ex dictis S. Thomæ, Johannis Nider aliorumque Doctorum
Catholicorum atque ex sermonibus Sensatis ac denuo cum
magno labore revisi.—Argentine, Arte et impensis* Johannis
Reynardi (alias Gruninger), 1489. [cf. Hain, 8509]

J. Nider was a German Dominican Friar and Inquisitor, flourished
in the University of Vienna, Deputy at the Council of Basle, died
at Nuremburg in 1438. (Du Pin *Eccles. History*, 15th century.)

15

SERMONES Pomærii de tempore (pars æstivalis) comportati
per fratrem Pelbartum de Themeswar professum divi Ordinis
S. Francisci collecti. Printed at Lugdunum by John Cleyn
[1489]. The sermons are numbered up to LXXX.

With these Sermons are bound in the same volume

POMÆRIUM Sermonum De Sanctis [pars hiemalis]. Numbered up to XCVII. [Hain, 12554]

Both volumes of Sermons are evidently the work of the same
printer, and were intended to be bound together. The Sermons
"de Sanctis" are without the names of place or printer, and those
"de Tempore" are without date: but at the end of the XCVII.
Sermon "de Sanctis" occurs

" Finis est partis : laus Christo gloria sanctis
Amen sit cordis Deo sit operis simul oris
Bis sep cent actis ocdonis ter tribus annis,"

which gives the date of 1489. This book seems to have been in
the possession of Ralph Thoresby and also of Wm. Herbert,
and has their respective autographs on the title page of the
Sermons "de Tempore" which runs, "Pomerium Sermonum de

Sanctis [instead of de Tempore] pars æstivalis." About twelve
leaves at the end of the book are more or less water-stained, otherwise it is in good condition, though somewhat wormed.

16

SERMONES Pomerii de Tempore comportati per fratrem
Pelbartum de Themeswar:—impressi per Henricum Grannum,
1502 (on vellum-like paper). iii. nonas Augusti. [Hain, 12555]

17

CELEBERRIMI et omnium excellentissimi divini verbi decla-
matoris patris Gotschalci Holen ordinis Eremitarum Augustini
sacræ theologiæ lectoris excellentissimi Sermones super Epistolas Pauli per anni circulum.

This book was printed at Hagenau by Henry Gran, 1517, in Gothic
type, and commences with an alphabetical table (containing seven
leaves) of the matter contained in the Dominical Sermons for the
winter season, seventy-four in number. To these sermons are
added two sermons in dialogue by John de Sancto Geminiano,
the first between Christ and the thief on his right hand on the
Cross, and the second between Christ and Cain, on the descent of
Christ "ad inferos." Next follows an alphabetical table, of nine
leaves, of the matter contained in the Sermons for the summer
season. Next, an alphabetical table, of one leaf, of the matter
contained in a treatise "de Dedicatione." Thirdly, an alphabetical table, of two leaves, of the order in which the Sermons
for the summer season occur. To the summer Sermons, one
hundred and seven in number, succeeds a Treatise on the Dedication, consisting (as may be gathered from the table) of
sixteen Sermons, but the latter part of the sixteenth is missing,
one leaf being torn out. At the end of the first table there is
a note "Ad Lectorem," to the effect that these Sermons were
considered so profound and instructive that John Rynman, principal bookseller at Hagenau, had them printed at his own expense
by Henry Gran. It is evident from the frequent marginal notes
that the book has been much studied, the sermons being replete
with curious and quaint stories, some of which are adopted by
Shakspeare, as "King Lear" in Sermon VI. of the winter series.
Many of them are derived from Bercorius' "Gesta Romanorum."

18

CARACCIOLUS (Robert de Licio) Sermones de laudibus

Sanctorum, Peter Drach, Spire, 1490. (On vellum-like paper.)
[Hain, 4484]

> This book is in clean, excellent condition, and once belonged to the
> Duke of Sussex. According to Gesner (Biblioth. p. 739) there
> was an edition of these Sermons printed also in 1490 by Nicholas
> Keslur, at Basle. Robert de Licio was born at Licio, and was
> Bishop of Aquino and of Licio.

20

POSTILLA super Evangelia dominicalia. "Hoc Volumen im-
pressuum est Moguntiæ circa Annum MCCCCL ab ipsis inventor-
ibus artis typographicæ et quidem ut existimo antequam impri-
menda Biblia et antequam detectum secretum quo artem velabant.
Et ideo deest mentio Urbis, Typographiæ et temporis. Hæc
editio incognita fuit omnibus qui de artis typographicæ inventione scripserunt, et est rarissima."

> When these letters are taken in detail and compared one with
> another it is manifest that they did not proceed from the same
> *matrix* nor consequently from the same *punch*. It may be that
> the historians of the art of printing have not seen this work,
> and many others which are without date, printer's name or
> place, and are not aware of the perfection the inventors had
> attained in this particular.
> This edition is certainly effected by involuted letters. There is
> scarcely a page in which there are not disarrangements of the
> letters in words, sometimes by some letters being higher, others
> lower than those which immediately precede or succeed them,
> so that the lines are sometimes unlevel and in others the letters
> are unequal in size or not of the same height. Three different
> alphabets are observable in this volume, one as regards capital
> letters, and one forming the titles at the head of the text, and
> a third of a smaller kind for the Gloss. It appears to me that this
> book was printed before the first *Bible*, and before the first *Catho-
> licon* with moveable letters. The paper bears the felegram of the
> papers used by the first printers, *i.e.* the head of an ox (see the leaf
> which has "explicit super Epulum dedicationis"). It is probable
> that the difference that may be observed in the form of the same
> letters is occasioned by the circumstance that the first printers cut
> their punches for entire syllables, of which the letters could not
> be perfectly like to those that were isolated, and that issued from
> a different matrix.

Description of a Book "inter rariores rarissimum."

TAXE Cancellaric apostolice et taxe sacre penitentiaræ itidem apostolicæ. The printer's device [St. Denis (headless) and his two companions]. Venundantur Parisiis in vico Sancti Jacobi ad crucem ligneam prope Sacellum Divi Ivonis per cossanum Denis bibliopolam cum descriptione Italæ ac cōpendio Universitatis Parisiensis et taxis beneficiorum ecclesiasticorū Regni Franciæ, 1520. Cum privilegio trienni.

> At the upper part of the title page are woodcuts of the papal arms (those of Leo X.) on a shell enclosed in a square, and parallel to these are the arms of France. On the reverse is the royal license to the printer, and a notice "Ad Lectorem," giving an account of this edition of the Taxæ. Then follow three leaves of table. The book of forty-two leaves is printed in Gothic type, and on the last leaf is a list of "errata post prelum emendanda" finishing with two lines of verse "Ad lectorem benevolum."

21

LEGENDA hæc aurea nitidis excutitur formis claret . . . plurimum censoria castigatione, usque adeo ut nihil perperam adhibitum remotumve quod ad rem potissimum pertinere non videatur offendi possit.

> Below this title is a wood engraving of the crucifixion of our Lord, and figures on each side, then the words "Venundantur Lugduni a Johanne honet ejusdem civitatis bibliopola prope sanctum eligium;" the whole enclosed in an engraved border representing personages of the Old and New Testament and legendary history. At the back of the title-page and on the seven following leaves is a table of matter contained in the volume, and, secondly, a list of the names of the persons whose legends the book records. The colophon gives the name of Stephen Balam as printer, and the date as 26th August, 1510. This book is by Jacobus de Voragine, and has been many times printed.

23

LEGENDA SANCTORUM, quæ collegit in unum Frater Jacobus matroni Januensis Ordinis Fratrum Predicatorum. Colophon at the end of 318th leaf: "Explicit legenda Lombardica Jacobi de Voragine, Ordinis Predicatorum Episcopi Januensis." On the 319th leaf begins "Sequuntur quædam legenda ac quibusdam aliis superaddita. Et primum de decem millibus Martyrum." At the end of the Appendix, which extends to leaf 369, occurs, "Lombardica historia explicat Anno Domini MCCCCLXXXI."

There is no name of place or printer; there are no signatures, but each leaf (369 in all, beside those of the table) is numbered by old Roman numerals. The table occupies 13 leaves. This book is not described by any bibliographer so far as I can find, but is a fine specimen of old typography, and is in excellent condition, with a good broad margin, though slightly water-stained as regards the earlier leaves. Printed in single column, 41 lines in a page.

25

JOHANNES DE FONTE (lector in Monte Pessulano) Compendium librorum Sententiarum quatuor in modum Conclusionum Sententialiter compositum. [Hain, 7225]

A specimen of very early printing, without signatures, date, name of place or printer, but assigned to Gunther Zainer, who printed in Augsburg from 1471—1484. As the book is without signatures the printing would be regarded as *before* 1484.

26

PARATUS de tempore continens Evangeliorum de tempore expositiones necnon de tempore Epistolarum Sermones. Sermones etiam de Sanctis. [Hain 12398]

This volume is printed on vellum-like paper, with signatures, but without date, printer's name or place; but is assigned by Gesner (*Biblioth.* p. 651) to "Argentine, 1487."

27

GALENSIS. Communiloquium sive summa collationum. [Hain, 7440]

This is in good condition (very slightly touched by the worm in one or two places), and is without signatures, printer's name or place. It is printed on vellum-like paper, with a broad margin, and is an early specimen of printing, probably by John Zainer of Ulm, 1481.

28

SERMONES Dominicales ex Epistolis et Evangeliis atque de Sanctis secundum Ecclesiæ Ordinem Wilhelmi, Cancellarii Parisiensis. Expensis Frederici Meyerberger et ductu Johannis Ormar, feria tertia "Invocavit" Anno 99 [1499].

This book is printed on vellum-like paper, and is in excellent condition, although a few of the leaves at the beginning are slightly water-stained.

29

TRES SERMONES Fratris Roberti, sc. De Annunciatione Virginis Marie: de prædestinato numero damnorum et de Cathenis.

Printed on vellum-like paper (by John Koelhoff?), without date, signature, or name of place or printer. These Sermons seem to be the remnant of a larger volume, but are beautiful specimens of early printing.

30

SERMONES Dominicales cum Expositionibus Evangeliorum per Annum satis notabiles et utiles omnibus Sacerdotibus Pastoribus et Capellanis qui alio nomine *"Dormi secure"* vel *"Dormi sine curâ"* sunt nuncupati eo quod absque magno studio faciliter possint incorporati et populo prædicati.

This book is a very good specimen of early typography, has signatures, but is without date, name of place or printer, paging, or other marks of more modern printed books. The water-mark on the paper is the figure of a *sickle:* and Dr. Kloss, a former owner of this book refers the printing to "Conradus de Homborch of Colonia, 1480:" giving references to *Panzer* i. 339, 466: *De le Vall.* i. 244. It is printed in double columns each containing 38 lines, with broad and clean margins.

A copy formerly belonging to the Duke of Sussex with signatures, but no printer's name, place or date, is assigned to John Koelhoff de Lubeck, printer at Cologne, 1481, and has the Sermons "de Sanctis" as well as "Dominicales". A fine specimen of paper printing. Dr. Bacon says Richard Maidstone is the author.

30*a*

SERMONES Dominicales.

Another copy, formerly belonging to the Duke of Sussex, with

signatures, but no printer's name, date or place, but in a note
in the cover is assigned to John Koelhoff de Lubeck, printer at
Cologne, 1483. The book is in good condition, printed in bold
type, in single columns, 39 lines, with good margins. In the
same volume are bound

SERMONES PEREGRINI, de Tempore, de Sanctis : with
the following note at the end, in much larger type: "Fratris
Perigrini In regionem divine pagine peregre proficiscentis doctoris clarissimi de tempore sanctisque per circulum anni sermones populares diligenter correcti hic finem comprehendunt
feliciter." [Hain, 12580]

This part has signatures, but without pagination, or date, or printer.
Single column, 40 lines in a column, and is evidently by the same
printer.

31

GUIDONIS DE MONTE ROTHERII, Manipulus Curatorum,
printed at Cologne. [Hain, 8169]

This early edition has signatures, but is without printer's name.
The Bibliographers do not mention any edition of this book as
printed at Cologne, but all early editions are very rare. (See
Ebert. ii. 691.)

32

FRATRIS Petri Berchorii Pictavensis Morale reductorium
super totam Bibliam quatuor et triginta libris consummatum
singulisque (secundum materiæ exigentiam) capitibus aptissime
distinctum, &c. Printed by Peter Langendorff, 21 Augt.,
1515.

33

VITA et Processus sancti Thomæ Cantuariensis Martyris
super Libertate ecclesiastica (4to) by John of Salisbury.
Colophon: Explicit quadripartita Historia continens passionem
sanctissimi Thomæ martyris Archepiscopi Cantuariensis et
Primatis Anglici una cum processu ejusdem super ecclesiastica
libertate quæ impressa fuit Parisiis per Magistrum Johannem
Philipi commorantem in vico Sancti Jacobi ad intersignium

Sanctæ Barbaræ, et completa Anno Domini Millesimo quadragentisimo nonagesimo quinto vicesima Septima Mensis Martii.

Between this Colophon and the Table occur four Epistles, two of them from S. Ignatius to S. John the Evangelist, one from that Bishop to the blessed Virgin Mary, and the remaining one from the Virgin to S. Ignatius. After the table is added a Treatise on Ecclesiastical jurisdiction described as follows in the Colophon: "Explicit quidam libellus de jurisdictione ecclesiastica factus per dominum Petrum Bertrandi et in concilio convenientibus prælatis regni Franciæ verbotenus in Gallia per ipsum deputatum ex parte ipsorum Prelatorum recitatus. Impressus Parisii per Magistrum Johannem Philippi Alemanius, In vico S. Jacobi ad intersignium Sanctæ Barbaræ Anno Domini Millesimo quadragentisimo nonagesimo quinto. Secunda Aprilis." An excellent specimen of early printing, clean, and in calf gilt, modern binding. [See Hain, 15510]

34

NOTALISSIMUS Quadragesimale et in toto suo processu tem. .... editum a quodam sacræ paginæ professore Ordinis prædicatorum Leonardo Italico quod a suo auctore "Sertum Fidei" intitulatur eo quod in eo omnes Articuli fidei luculentissime sparsim per sermones declarantur.

This book is a fine specimen of early printing on vellum-like paper with signatures, but without pagination, name of printer, place or date. Prefixed to the Sermons is a list of the Sermons contained in the volume, and at the close an index of the matter contained in each sermon. The Sermons finish with the following Colophon: "Finitum est hoc egregium et perutile quadragesimale editum a fratre Leonardo Italico sacre theologiæ professore quod valde utile est omnibus predicatoribus homines ad virtutes hortari a vitiis retrahere volentibus. Deo gratias." This seems probably the edition mentioned by Maittaire as printed at   . It has remarkably clean, broad margins. The printing is in double columns of 38 lines. Bound in the same volume is the first edition of Cassian.

34a

CASSIANI Collationes Sanctorum patrum.

A splendid book on vellum, without signature, pagination, name of printer, or date, but said to have been printed at Bruxelles by the Brothers of the Common life about 1474. (See Ebert. *Biblioth.*

vol. i. p. 276) in large 4to. in Gothic letters in two columns of 38 lines. The book is very scarce. In strength of type and size of letters the text is like that of Ulrich Zell, of Cologne.

36

SERMONES Discipuli de tempore et Sanctis, de Dedicatione ecclesie, Quadragesimale, exemplorum, casus Papales et epis-copales, Inhibitiones a sacra communione, Promptuarium, De Miraculis beate Marie Virginis. Printed at Nuremberg by Johannes Stuchs, 7th March, 1517. Folio.

This book has an engraved well-executed title page, representing St. Jerome sitting at a writing table in the act of writing. On the floor close to the table opposite to him is a sleeping lion. The book is perfect and in good condition, with a copious table of the matter contained in it, and affords a good specimen of the press from which it issued. It is printed in double columns, 72 lines in a column.

37

SERMONES Discipuli de Tempore et de Sanctis una cum Promptuario Exemplorum et de miraculis beatæ Virginis (folio). Colophon: Finit opus perutile simplicibus Curam Animarum gerentibus per venerabilem et devotum Johannem Herolt sancti Dominici sectatorem professum de Tempore et de Sanctis cum Promptuario Exemplorum atque Tabulis suis collectum. "Discipulus nuncupatur Impressum Argentinæ in officina Martin Flaech junioris cura ejusdem Anno Domini MCCCCCIII. pridie nonas Octobres.

This edition of a book very often reprinted is in a complete state, in modern binding, and in good condition except as regards a slight water-stain which yet in no way interferes with the printed text. The Promptuarium is not often printed with the Sermons. There are blank spaces left to admit of illuminated capitals throughout the whole book.

38

OPUS præclarum Sermonem Socci de Tempore sic dictorum cum de suco id est de medulla sacræ paginæ stilo subobscuro exquisitissime sint collecti. Printed at Strasburgh 4th Feb., 1484, by John de Grüninger. [Hain, 14826]

This book is in good condition, having a clear, broad margin. The first part contains one hundred and twenty-seven sermons from Advent to Easter, and one hundred and twenty-five from Easter to the end of the Ecclesiastical division of the year. The book has signatures and a kind of running title and pagination in the form of "Sermo primus," "Secundus," &c. up to "Nonus," after that number the pagination takes the form of "Sermo X.," &c. The type is a fine specimen of the Strasburgh press. The watermark is the ox's head. Prefixed to the book is an alphabetical Register of the matters contained in the volume, and secondly, one of the subject matter contained in the Sermons as they occur in the volume.

42

DIALOGUS qui vocatur Scrutinium Scripturarum compositus per reverendum patrem dominum Paulum de Sancta Maria Magistrum in Theologia Episcopum Burgensem Archicancellarium serenissimi principis Domini Regis Castellæ et Legionis. [An. 1470.] [See Hain, 10762]

This book is a good specimen of the early Mantuan press, of which there are not many to be commonly met with. It is in good condition except that some of the leaves are slightly wormed, but not so as to interfere with the printing. The last few leaves are wanting, and with them the Colophon: but this, the first and scarce edition of the work, was printed at Mantua by John Schell, or Schall, from 1475—1479 (see *Biblioth. Vet. Hispan.* vol. ii. p. 239, Madrid, 1788), and is without signatures or pagination.

43

VIOLA SANCTORUM (in a bold letter, on a fly leaf) small 4to. Colophon: Viola Sanctorum finit feliciter Anno Domini MCCCCLXXXI. kal. Julii Nurembergæ impressum satis emendatum elaboratumque.

This book is in good Gothic type, has spaces left for the initial capitals, but has no printer's name. A few of the leaves at the beginning of the book are somewhat water-stained, and a few toward the end very slightly wormed. Probably printed by Ant. Coburger.

44

DIRECTORIUM Concubinariorum saluberrimum quo quædam
stupenda et quasi inaudita pericula quam apertissime resol-
vuntur nedum Clericis ut etiam Laicis hoc crimine pollutis
necessarium, sed et communi populo præsertim erga sacerdotes
concubinarios quam utilissimum ob infinitos laqueos quibus
tam ipsi quam indoctum vulgus propter ipsos irretirentur
(small 4to. in Gothic type). Therentius Veritas odium parit
Esdras Sed justo sub judice vincit. At the end of the table
there is the following notice: "Impressum est hoc Directorium
concubinatorum primitum Agripine alias Colonie nunc post
virgineum partum MCCCCCVIII. et jam denuo ibidem anno
sequenti MDIX. in officina literaria ingenuorum librorum
Quentell."

This curious book, intended as a guide to Confessors in their dealings
with lay and clerical fornicators, consists of xxxi. leaves besides
the fly-leaf, which serves for a title-page, and three leaves of table
at the end: on the reverse of the last leaf of the table are some
verses addressed to persons of the class treated of. The paging
forms a kind of running title, the numbers up to 18 being written
at length, after 18 the leaves bear the Roman numerals.

46

SERMONES collecti a fratre Jordano de Quedlinburg, Lectore
Magdeburgensi Ordinis fratrum Eremitarum Sancti Augustini.
Printed by John de Gruninger, 28 March, 1484. [Hain, 9440]

This Book is in excellent condition, printed on vellum-like paper,
and formerly belonged to Robert Southey, whose autograph and
book-plate it bears. The water-mark is the ox's head.

47

BAPTISTÆ Mantuani Carmelitæ de Patientia aurei libri tres
(small 4to.) 1499. Nihil sine causa Olpe. Coloph. Impressum
Basiliæ opera Johannis Bergman de Olpe XVI. kl. Septembres
Anno Salutis MCCCCLXXXIX. principante Domino Maximiliano
cui salus et victoria. Amen. Then follow some complimentary
verses addressed to Wymmar, Dean of Ercklens, but then
Deacon of Agria. [See Hain, 2407]

The book is printed in Roman type, and is perhaps one of the earliest specimens of that type used by the printers at Basle except Froben: it is also in good condition considering that it is in the original boards. It is without any pagination.

48

HYSTORIA Ecclesiastica. The colophon: Eusebii Cæsariensis ecclesiastica finit hystoria per Magistrum Goffredum Boussardum sacræ theologiæ doctorem eximium exactissime correcta et emendata diligentia Petri Levet Parisii impressa expensis Johannis de Combelens et prœfati Levet, Anno 1497, pridie kalendas Septembres. Double columns, 46 lines. [Hain, 6713]

Bound in the same volume is

CASSIODORI Senatoris viri dei de regimine ecclesiæ primitivæ hystoria tripartita feliciter incipit. The colophon: Historiæ ecclesiasticæ explicit liber duodecimus et ultimus Gloria Individuæ Trinitati, pax legentibus, Credulitas audientibus, Vita facientibus. Amen. [Hain, 4570]

Both books are on vellum paper excellent specimens of printing, especially *Cassiodorus*, in good and perfect condition, and with Monograms of the respective printers on their title pages. Both are in 4to. double columns, 54 lines. [I do not find the *Monogram* of the printer of *Cassiodorus*, nor the date, nor any account of the edition.]

49

MAGISTRI Roberti Holkot super quatuor libros Sententiarum questiones (8vo. in Gothic type). Colophon: Hujus operis diligenter impressi Lugduni a Magistri Johanni Cleyn Alemanus, anno salutis nostræ M. [quincentesimo decimo] (1510) ad Idus Aprilis. [cf. Hain, 8763]

A former possessor of this book seems to have tried to obliterate the date except the "m", but the date was 1510. The book is in a very legible small Gothic type, on vellum paper, and in the original binding: but in form, texture, &c. is a reprint of the *same Treatise* of the *same Author*, by the same printer, Cleyn, in 1505, now in my possession. The type, paper, &c. of the edition of 1505 is also of a better quality, only that the blank spaces left in 1505 for initial capitals are occasionally supplied by engraved capitals in 1510. In condition, &c. the edition of 1505 is a very handsome book in all respects.

OPUS praeclarissimum eximii Magistri Roperti Holket sacræ
theologiæ moralissimi atque doctissimi professoris Ordinis fratrum prædicatorum super Sapientiam Salomonis quam Philo
collegit. Printed at Spire by Peter Drach, 1483, 4th kalend.
of March. [Hain, 8756]

The book is in good condition, with signatures but without pagination. The blank spaces left for illuminated initial letters are not
filled up. After the colophon there follows the printer's device,
viz., two shields suspended from the branch of a tree, that on the
left hand containing a Wivel, the other a pine tree with a star on
each side. Temperley (*Hist. of Printing*, p. 124) states that the
device of two shields, in one of which were three stars, was that
used by Faust and Schoeffer, the printers at Mentz.
N.B. Maittaire (i. 4, Amsterdam, 1733) observes that the name of
Faust and Schoeffer does not appear in books beyond 1470; nor
Schoeffer alone beyond 1492.

SERMONES dominicales super Epistolas Pauli et consequenter
per circulum anni egregii domini doctoris Magistri Thomæ
de Haselbach in Austria (Prima pars). [Hain, 8370]

This book is a thick folio, in excellent condition, and is a fine
specimen of early printing. It is without signatures, paging,
or printer's name or place; but at the end the following colophon
occurs: "Explicit prima pars Sermonum super Epistolas Pauli
Anno Domini MCCCCLXXVIII die XIII Decembris iii." The capitals
are illuminated, but are of the simplest description. The initial
A to the prologue to the Sermons is an elaborate kind of woodcut,
representing our Lord washing S. Peter's feet (S. John xiii. 9),
and was evidently a block-printed initial intended for every copy
of that edition of the Sermons. The prevailing paper-mark is
a snail carrying its shell. It is finally to be observed that this
book seems to have been printed with moveable types, not with
blocks, for in most pages *letters* occur in words which shew
them to have been *single* letters, *e.g.* on the first page, line seven
from the bottom, the word "*considerandum*" was manifestly
printed with types that were distinct one from the other, and not
united: so also as regards the words "*animarum curam*" in the
next line.

D. DIONYSII Carthusiani insigne commentariorum opus, in
Psalmos omnes Davidicos, &c. Accedit ad hæc ejusdem in

matutinalia VII Cantica in Magnificat quoque, Nunc Dimittis, &c. Parisiis. Apud Johannem Roigny, via ad D. Jacobum sub Basilico et quatuor elementis. 1542.

The book is in good condition, and is in old monastic binding. Below the title-page is a representation of the printer at his press. It is printed at Paris by Louis Tiletan. At the top of the press is printed "*Prelum ascensianum.*"

Bound with this is

D. DIONYSII Carthusiani Piæ ac eruditæ enarrationes in Librum Jobi, Tobiæ, Judith, Hester, Esdrae, Nehemiæ, 1 Machabæorum, 2 Machabæorum. Coloniæ, impensis Petri Quentell. Anno MDXXXIIII, Mense Martio.

This part has a handsomely engraved title-page, the upper part representing God's threatened judgment against the enemies of his church; the lower part, the prophet interceding against its fulfilment. [Cf. Panzer vi. 427.]

PHARETRA, auctoritates et dicta SS. Doctorum, Philosophorum et Poetarum ordine alphabetico deposita continens. Printed at Argentorati by John Mentelin, 1470 (Panzer i. 73, 413). [Hain, 12908]

This book is denominated *Pharetra* "because like as the quiver of archers is provided with various kinds of arrows, by which, as opportunity serves, an enemy may wound or kill his foe, so in this book will be found various and potent sayings of holy doctors, and other philosophers and poets, by which our ancient enemy, the devil, may be kept at bay whenever he desires to overcome the sinner."

This book is an exceedingly fine copy, and is the first edition. It is without signature, pagination, name of printer or place, but a MS. note in the handwriting of a practised scribe states that the book was purchased for the Monastery of S. Ægidius in Nuremburg of the Order of S. Benedict. The book contains, first, after some introductory observations, an alphabetical list of names of authors quoted, also an alphabetical list of subjects treated of in the book, these consisting of six leaves; then follows the subject of the work, occupying 349 leaves, double columns, 50 lines in each column.

SUMMA quæ vocatur Catholicon de Janua, sc. Johan. de Balbis. [Hain, 2251]

This book is large folio, fine, clean copy, with broad margin, and contains 391 leaves in two columns, with 58 lines in a full column, without signatures, catch-words, pagination, name of place, printer or date. Type remarkable and fine, on vellum-like paper, the paper-mark being a rose. In a manuscript note at the end of the Dresden copy of this edition of the Catholicon the date 1482 is assigned as the year in which it was printed, but it was probably at a somewhat earlier date (see Panzer iv. 93, Eber. ii. 837).

PLURA et diversa et inestimabilis doctrinæ atque utilitatis Divi Aurelii Augustini Sermonum opera: nuper summa cura et diligentia Udalrici Gering et magistri Berchtoldi Rembolt sociorum quam emendatissime impressa apud solem aureum in vico Sorbonico Parisiis venalia comperies, quorum nomine eo ordine quo in hoc continentur volumine hic annotata sunt. Ad fratres in Heremo commorantes Sermones lxxvi. De Verbis domini, Sermones lxiiii. De Verbis Apostoli, Ser. xxv. In Epistolam Canonicam beati Johannis primam Sermones x. Homiliæ id est Sermones populares, Quinquaginta. In Evangelium secundum Johannem Tractatus cxxiiii. De tempore Sermones cclvi. De Sanctis Sermones li. [See Hain, 2007]

On the reverse of this title is an engraving representing S. Augustine in the act of copying into a book from certain volumes held open to him by the pope and a crowd of cardinals, all of whom are seated: the device of the printer Rembolt being on the title-page. The book is perfect, having a running pagination, and contains 415 leaves, numbered including the index, or "Emporium" of the Sermons with which the book commences, and the "Annotatio Sermonum de Sanctis" which concludes it. The date does not appear, but it is known that Gering, the printer of this volume, introduced the art of printing into Paris in 1470, and had Rembolt and others as partners: that Gering and his associates removed from the Sorbonne in 1473, and that his name alone appears in books printed by him subsequently to 1477. Now as this book was printed whilst Gering and his associates remained in the Sorbonne it must have been printed between 1470 and 1473 (see Palmer, *Hist. of Print.* p. 165 and seq.; Temperley, *Hist. of*

Print. p. 132). As regards Gering's works they are looked upon as among the best specimens of printing of their time. This book is in excellent condition, and in old binding.

SPECULUM EXEMPLORUM. Ad laudem et gloriam sempiternæ individuæque Trinitatis beatissimæ Mariæ Virginis Omnium Sauctorum et Angelorum, finitum et completum est hoc Speculum exemplorum per me Richardum Paefroed civem Daventriensem in crastino beatissimorum Apostolorum Philippi et Jacobi Anno Dni MCCCCLXXXI. De quo sit Deus benedictus in sæcula. Amen. [Hain, 14915]

A fine specimen of the work of the first known printer at Daventer. The book is quite perfect except as regards the last two leaves, which are injured by the damp, but happily the above written colophon is uninjured. The *prologus* gives a curious account of the object for which the *Speculum* was completed, and the sermons from which the matter composing it was collected.

OPUS preclarum omnium omeliarum et postillarum venerabilium ac egregio eorum doctorum gregorii, augustini, iheronimi, ambrosii, bede, herici, leonis, maximi, johannis episcopi, atque origenis integraliter super evangelia dominicalia de tempore et de sanctis pro totius anni circulum cum quibusdam eorundem sparsim interpositis sermonibus hinc inde suis locis collectis et coaptatis temporibus, in partem hyemalem ac estivalem divisum incipit feliciter. Pars hyemalis et prima.

This volume contains the Homilies " in partem hycmalem" which were collected by Paul the Deacon at the command of Charlemagne, for the use of the Clergy and Religious in his dominions. That monarch's letter, explaining the object he had in view in this collection of Homilies is prefixed as a prologue to the work. The volume contains 255 leaves.

The following is the title of the Homilies " in partem estivalcm :"

OMILIE et postilla venerabilium doctorum gregorii, augustini, iheronymi, ambrosii, bede, hereci, leonis et maximi integraliter super evangelia per æstatem cum quibusdam sermonibus eorundem sparsim interpositis incipiunt feliciter. Pars estivalis. The following is the colophon to this part: Expliciunt omelie super evangelia de tempore et de sanctis per totum annum cum quibusdam sermonibus eorundem admisse et approbate ab alma universitate coloniensi impresse autem per me Conradum de homborch ad laudem et gloriam dei qui est semper benedictus in secula. Amen. [See Hain, 8792]

This book consists of 288 leaves, the paging, which is by a later hand, being continued from the other volume. In the first part 80 is put for 79, and 178 for 177; in the second part 378 is put for 377, while *two* leaves are numbered 458, but in all these cases there is no defect in those places in which these errors of the scribe occur. The books are printed in double columns, consisting of 40 lines. Both volumes are clean and in excellent condition, with broad margins; are without signatures, pagination or date, but are evidently very good specimens of Conrad's printing, who was the father of the press at Cologne, having commenced his printing as early as 1470, soon after which time may probably be the date of these books, which it is believed are a first edition. They are in good monastic binding. Respecting the rarity of specimens of this printer's works, see Dibdin's *Bibliotheca Spenceriana*, vol. iii. pp. 430, &c.

SCOTUS, on the first book of the Sentences, which is thus described in the colophon: Explicit Scriptum super Primum Sententiarum editum a fratre Johanne Duns Ordinis fratrum minorum Doctore subtilissimo ac omnium Theologorum principe. Per excellentissimum sacræ theologiæ doctorem Magistrum Thomam Pemcheth Anglicum Ordinis Eremitarum S. Augustini in famosissimo studio Patavino ordinarie legentem maxima cum diligentia emendatum. Impressum Venetiis, expensis et mandato Johannis de Colonia Sociique ejus Johannis Manthen de Gherretzem Anno a Natali Xtiano 1477 die vero 26 Julij. [Hain, 6416]

The work contains 262 leaves, of which 228 are numbered in an old hand; the text is in double columns of 51 lines each. The last 15 leaves are occupied with what may be called criticisms on the work, described in the following colophon: "Et sic est finis harum Additionum quæ secundum nonullorum opinionem textui doctoris subtilissimi super primum Sententiarum librum adduntur et in eodem locis suis interponuntur:" On this last leaf is printed a register of the catch-words of every leaf. The work has signatures and brief running title, but no pagination, except such as is supplied by a later hand, as far as p. 228. The book is in folio, in monastic binding, and is printed on beautiful vellum-like paper, with clean, broad margins, and double columns of 51 lines each, and is, taken altogether, as good a specimen of early printing as is to be met with. Respecting the printers of the work, Palmer observes that they were equal to any of their contemporaries in the fineness of their paper, and the elegance and correctness of their work (*Hist. of Print.* p. 146).

SCOTUS on the second book of the Sentences. Thus described in the colophon: Johannis Scoti Ordinis Minorum Sacræ theologiæ Professoris perexcellentissimi 2^0 super sententiarum quæstiones a Thoma Pemchet Anglico sacræ paginæ doctore clarissimo summa emendata cum diligentia finiunt feliciter. Necnon operate characterizateque sublimi librarum effigie ductu et impensis virorum circumspectorum domini Io. Agrippensis dominique Io. Manten de Gherretzem Sociorum. Anno Salutis 1478, 7 idus Januarii. [Hain, 6416]

This book consists of 142 leaves, then 8 pages of index, one containing a register of catch-words, followed by 6 leaves of extra conclusions, thus defined in a colophon: "Debet in fine omnium harum conclusionum Scoti poni illud extra quod est pro 6o. distinctione angelorum quorum principi deo fit laus et gloria per eterna secula. Amen."

Bound in the same volume are

QUODLIBETA, or miscellaneous questions, by Scotus, having the following colophon: Et sic est finis horum quodlibetorum a Johanne Duns Ordinis fratrum minorum Doctore subtillissimo omnium Theologorum principe, editorum per excellentissimum sacræ Theologiæ doctorum Magistrum Thomam Pancheth Anglicum Ordinis fratrum eremitarum S. Augustini famosissimo studio Patavino ordinarie legentem maxima cum diligentia emendatorum quorum bonitate ac emendatione diligenti impressa fuere Venetiis impensis Johannis de Colonia sociique ejus Johannis Manthen de Gherretzem. Anno MCCCCLXXVII die vero VII mensis Octobris. Laus Deo. [Hain, 6434]

These Quodlibets occupy 103 leaves, the four last consisting of the table of subjects, and the last leaf having the register of catch-words. It will be noted that these Quodlibets were printed in 1477, while the second book on the Sentences was printed in 1478. In the character of the binding, and in the general condition, it corresponds in all respects with the first book on the Sentences.

SCOTUS, Commentary on the third book of the Sentences, described in the colophon as: Scriptum super 3o sententiarum editum a fratre Johanne duns ordinis fratrum minorum doctore subtillissimo, ac omnium theologorum principe. Per excellentissimum sacre theologie doctorem magistrum Thomam pencheth anglicum ordinis fratrum heremitarum sancti Augustini, in famosissimo studio Patavino ordinarie legentem; maxima cum diligentia emendatum. Impressum Venetiis ad expensas et mandatum Johannis de Colonia: sociique ejus Johannis manthen de Gherretzem. Anno domini 1477. Laus Deo. [Hain, 6416]

SCOTUS on the fourth book of the Sentences, is described in the colophon as follows: Johannis scoti in 4to sententiarum opus preclarissimum ceteris theologie voluminibus emendatis ac castigatis exscriptum. Idem autem diligentissime recognovit Thomas anglicus summus in theologia magister. Impressionique Venetiis deditum est ductu et impensa Johannis Colonie aggripinensis sociique ejus Johannis manthen de Gherretzem qui una fideliter degunt et cuncta ad communem utilitatem peragunt. [Hain, 6416]

Duns Scotus, on the third and fourth book of the Sentences, edited by Thomas Pancheth Anglicus (called "*Pemchett*" by Pitts, p.675), printed at Venice by John de Colonia and his partner, John Manthen de Gretzen. The date MCCCCLXXVII is added to the third part, but no date is affixed to the fourth part. There is this difference between the colophon of the third and fourth books, that the editor of the former is Thomas Pemchct Anglicus, in the latter it is simply Thomas Anglicus. The book is a fine specimen of the work of those celebrated printers, whether regard be paid to (vellum) paper, type, margin or original binding.

All the *tabulæ* and registers of the catch-words are perfect. It will be noted also that the commentaries on the several books of the Sentences were printed at different intervals of the year. This may be accounted for, as Pemchett printed the Commentary of Scotus at the request of his Auditory (Pitts ut supra).

PETRI RICHARDI artium et sacræ theologiæ Professoris optime meriti Sermonum opus super Epistolas et Evangelia totius Anni clarissimum multis probatorum authorum Sententiis et exemplis refertum (in two parts). Printed by Berthold Rembolt, "expensis Johannis Petit," 1518, on 12th August.

The title-page bears John Petit's device, the text on it is in red and black letters. The book is quite perfect, and is a very good specimen of the style of type then used. The number of leaves in the first part extends to 174, those of the second part to 162. The binding is old. Small 4to. [Panzer, viii. 45]

TRACTATUS Brevis et Utilis Infirmis Visitandis et Confessionem eorum Audiendis.

Black letter, 6 leaves, without date, name of printer or place, or signature; very early, probably about 1470. This is a direction for visiting, and a form of confession prescribed for the sick.

LEONARDI DE UTINO. Sermones quadragesimales de petitionibus super evangeliis totis Quadragesime Magistri Leonardi de Utino, ordinis fratrum predicatorum valde theologales: et complurimum omnibus Christi fidelibus pernecessarii usque hactenus impressi vigilanter visitati per fratrem Petrum de Tardito eiusdem ordinis et conventus Chamberiaci, sacre theologie professorem cum tabula in pagina sequenti inserta. Lugd. 1518, Johannem Marion.

The colophon states the book to be printed at Lyons by John Marion, 1518. The initial letter of the title page is well engraved, and at the foot is the well-known device of Marion. The book is printed in clear Gothic type, in double columns, 41 lines in a column, with running title. The initial capitals are engraved. Book in excellent condition, bound in green morocco. Small octavo.

SERMONUM floridorum fratris *Leonardi de Utino* sacræ theologiæ Professoris ac Ordinis Prædicatorum præcipui quos prædicavit Florentiæ (A.D. 1435) coram tota Curia Romana ibidem tunc temporis residente "Eugenio Papa" iv. (sm. 4to). [Hain, 16139]

> Printed at Lyons by John Trechsel, MCCCCXCVI. The book is quite perfect, is well printed, and at end has the printer's device: also in old binding.

SERMONES Fratris Gabrielis Barelete ordinis predicatorum tam quadragesimales et de Sanctis. Noviter impressi. Et ubi prius fuerunt interposita carmina Petrarche et Dantis in eorum vulgari modo per venerabilem Magistrum Johannem Anthonii ordinis minorum italicum sunt verbis latinis translata.

> The title is in Gothic characters. The colophon at the end of De Sanctis states it to have been printed at Lyons in 1502, by "Claud d'Avost alias de troie." The book contains Sermones Quadragesimales, et de Sanctis. This book has the autograph of Robert Southey. In this book the Sermones de Sanctis come first, the Quadragesimales second. At the dorsal of the title-page occurs a list of the saints who are commemorated. Prefixed to the Quadragesimal sermons is a preface by Benedictus Britianus, addressed to Thomas Caietan. [Panzer, vii. 278.] This is supposed to be the second edition of this now very uncommon book. The first is supposed to have been printed in Italy between 1495 and 1500. As regards the sermons themselves, they are described by Dupin as "full of impertinences and ridiculous things, unworthy of the gravity wherewith the word of God should be preached." See also a MS. note to the same effect on the fly-leaf of the book.

SERMONES Fratris Gabrielis Barlete ordinis predicatorum tam quadragesimales et de sanctis. Venales extant sub signo divi Claudii: in vico Sancti Jacobi.

> Between these two sentences is an engraved and rubricated bookseller's device.

> The colophon states that the book was printed in 1507 at Paris, "per Magistrum Johannem seurre alias de pica, expensis Francis Regnault." This book seems to have belonged to an earnest

Franciscan, since the same four leaves of the sermon on the Immaculate Conception have been cut out, as in the former edition.

D. DIONYSII Carthusiani in Evangelium Lucæ enarratio, &c. Parisiis. Apud Guillelmum le Bret. In clauso brunello sub signo cornu Cerui. 1548.

Printer's device, a tree with the motto, "Spes Mea Deus." The book is in Roman type. Small octavo.

ELUCIDISSIMA in Divi Pauli Epistolas commentaria *Dionysii*, olim Carthusiani apud celebrem Ruremundam ducatus Geldriæ urbem, cui in componendis sacrarum literarum libris vix alter similis successit.

With the Commentary are a life of the author, a catalogue of his works, and an epistle to Charles, duke of Gueldres. Printed by John Petit, Paris, 1531. Printer's device, two lions bearing a shield, on which is a fleur-de-lis, and the initials J. P.

IN SACROSANCTUM Jesu Christi Domini nostri evangelium secundum Joannem, pie erudite juxta Catholicam doctrinam Enarrationes, pro concione explicate. Anno Domini 1536 Moguntiæ. Accessit operi, eiusdem diui Joannis Apostoli Epistola prima, item pro concione non minus erudite quam pie enarrata, Moguntiæ in summa æde. Anno 1545. Per F. Joannem Ferum, summæ apud Mogunt. ædis Concionatorem, et cænobij D. Francisi Guardianum. Antverpiæ, Apud Mar. Nutium sub Cicionijs MDLVI. Cum regis Privilegio.

Ferus was a learned Roman Catholic divine who died in 1554. After his death his writings were expurgated by the congregation of the Index, as favouring too much the doctrine of the Reformation. This and other early editions are scarce. This volume is in monastic binding, and in good condition.

POSTILLÆ sive Conciones in Epistolas et Evangelia quæ ab Aduentu usque ad Pascha in Ecclesia legi consuerunt, authore R. patre D. Joanne Fero Concionatore absolutissimo interprete vero M. Joanne Gunthero. Pars Prima. Antverpiæ. In ædibus Joannis Steelfij, MDLV.

On title-page is printer's device. Small octavo.

REVERENDI Patris D. Joannis Feri in totam Genesim, non minus eruditæ quam Catholicæ enarrationes. Tertia Æditio. Coloniæ Agrippinæ Apud hæredes Arnoldi Birckmanni Anno MDLXII.

On the title-page is printer's device and name. In chap. viii., p. 248, this Romanist author, in a passage beginning, "In ecclesia autem, sacrificium nostrum est Christus," &c., describes our feeding on Christ in the Sacrament as held by the Church of England. Small octavo.

POSTILLÆ sive Conciones Reuerend. D. Johannis Feri Metropolitanæ Moguntinæ Concionatoris absoluti. In Epist. et Evang. de Sanctis quorum a Festo Paschæ usque ad Aduentum in Ecclesia Catholica celebratur memoria, Iam primum latinitati donatæ per M. Joan. a Via. Psalm xxxiv. Venite parvuli, audite me, timorem Domini docebo vos. Antverpiæ. In ædibus Joannis Stelsij, MDLXII. Cum Gratia et Privilegio.

On title-page is printer's device. Small octavo.

SERMONES dominicales super Evangelia et Epistolas de tempore hyemali: plurima scitu necessaria non solum divini verbi declamatoribus: verum etiam singulis christiane religionis cultoribus complectentes, editi a fratre Hugone de Prato Florido ordinis predicatorum: ac nuperrime summa diligentia castigati.

In a colophon at the end of pars hyemalis it is stated that it was printed in the officina literaria of Antonius du Ky at Lyons; but on the dorso of that colophon occurs the device of the Marescal press of Lyons.

The following is the title of the pars estivalis:

SERMONES dominicales super Evangelia et Epistolas de
tempore estivali quoque plurima scitu necessaria divini verbi
declamatoribus: ac etiam singulis christiane religionis cultoribus complectentes: editi a fratre Hugone de Prato Florido
Ordinis predicatorum: ac nuperrime (ut uni cuique patere
poterit) castigatiores redditi.

> The two parts are in one volume, with an engraved title the same
> in both, a congregation addressed by a preacher. The date of
> each part is 1528. The first title having been partially mutilated
> is mounted. There is no table to the first part. The book is well
> printed, but partly water-stained; in other respects it is in good
> condition.

FUNDAMENTUM aureum omnis anni sermonum magistri
N. de Gorra ordinis prædicatorum tam fructuose tamque curiose
distinctum ut cum omnibus anni evangeliis et epistolis sanctorum etiam historias generaliterque occurentes materias plene
pulcerrimeque sustineat atque distinguat. Then follows printer's device with the name M. N. de la Barre, and below,
Venales hos invenies in Coronato lilio vico sancti Jacobi
[Paris].

> Gorran flourished A.D. 1400. The book consists of 202 folios in
> small 8vo, followed by three leaves of table of matter, the first
> page of the table being printed on the dorsal of folio 202; a fourth
> and last leaf of the table being apparently missing. The book
> is printed in double columns, 42 lines in each, with running title;
> it is in good condition, in old monastic binding.

1. SERMONES quadragesimales fratris Guillelmi Pepin novo
ordine ab ipso authore digesti: decretales scilicet casibus (qui
hactenus separati fuerant) suis quibusque Evangeliis coaptatis.

> These sermons consist of short and succinct expositions of the
> Epistles and Gospels, read during the quadragesimal season.
> Those on the Epistles take up 140 leaves, the sermons on the
> Gospels occupy 352 leaves. This is the first edition the author
> issued from the office of John Petit in Paris, 1529, the sermons
> on the Epistles being printed in the October of that year, those

on the Gospels in the January following. The title-page is got
up in John Petit fashion, and the book (in French calf binding,
vellum paper) is a beautiful specimen of printing and in excellent
condition. [W. Pepin was a Dominican monk of the reformed
convent of S. Louis, at Evreux.] Small octavo.

2. SERMONES quadraginta de destructione Nineve hoc est,
omnis Generis vitiorum, authore fratre Guillelmo Pepin sacre
theologie professore optime merito. Parisiis.
Printed at Paris by Claude Chevallon, 1527.

HISTORIA SCHOLASTICA. Magistri Petri Comestoris
Historia Scholastica magnam sacræ scripturæ partem, quæ et
in serie et in glossis crebro diffusa erat, breviter complectens.
Mendis omnibus post omnes omnium hactenus editiones seclu-
sis, in lucem exit cum optimis capitulorum quotationibus in
margine decenter appositis, excusa Lugduni MCCCCXXXIIII.
[See Hain, 5530]
> The title-page is engraved, and contains a representation of the
> author in his cell. The book is in square 8vo, consisting of 255
> leaves, printed in double columns, 52 lines in a column, with
> engraved capitals; it has signatures, and is paged in Roman
> numerals. Printed at Lyons by Nicolas Petit and Hector Penet.
> This book was formerly the property of the Duke of Sussex.

SERMONES Discipuli de Tempore et de Sanctis.
> Without printer's name, date or place. Small quarto or octavo.
> Evidently not of an early date, and by a former possessor is
> conjectured to have been printed at Nuremberg about 1514.
> The type is in small neat Gothic letter, in double columns, with
> 57 lines in a column, and with running title. The earlier pages
> are somewhat water-stained, otherwise the book is in good con-
> dition, and a good specimen of printing for the time. It may
> be noted of these Sermons that they were made up of the sayings
> of pious men (saints), as collected out of different authors by
> John Herolt, who usually styles himself Discipulus. Among the
> authors quoted are Beda, Bernard, Gregory, and of later writers,
> Gorram, Symon de Cassia, M. Raymundus, Innocent Hostiensis,
> with many others.

PROPUGNACULUM Ecclesie adversus Lutheranos: pe
Judocum Clichtoveum Neopostuensem, doctorem theologum
elaboratum; et tres libros continens.

> Then follows a recital of what is contained in each book. On the
> dorsal of the title-page commences a letter (the initial of which
> is engraved) to Louis Guillard, Bishop of Chartres. The colophon
> states that it was printed at Cologne by Jerome Alopecius, 1526.
> The book is in small octavo, 309 leaves, running title; the index
> of contents, and a second alphabetical index of the matter contained
> in the book, consisting of 23 leaves, are at the end of the book.
> This is probably the first edition of the Propugnaculum, and like
> all the early editions of books connected with the Lutheran
> controversy is correspondently rare. It is in handsome monastic
> binding, and is in excellent condition.

CONCILIORUM quatuor generalium Nicæni, Constantinopoli-
tani, Ephesini et Calcedonensis. Que divus Gregorius magnus
tanquam quatuor evangelia colit ac veneratur. Tomus primus
Quadraginta quoque septem Conciliorum provincialium authen
ticorum. Decretorum etiam sexaginta novem pontificum, ab
apostolis et eorundem canonibus, vsque ad Zachariam primum
Isidoro Authore. Item Bulla Aurea Caroli iiii., Imperatoris
de electione regis Romanorum. Parisiis, Apud Franciscum
Regnault, 1535.

The following is the title of the second volume:

TOMUS Secundus Conciliorum generalium. Practica quinte
synodi Constantinopolitane, Fo. i. Sexta synodus Constan-
tinopolitana, Fo. xlii. Acta concilii Cōstantiēsis, Fo. cii. Decreta
cōcilii Basiliensis, Fo. cliii. Approbatio actor cōcilii Basiliē
per Nicolaū papā quintū, Fo. ccxvi. Confirmatio constitu-
tionum Frederici et Karoline, Fo. ccxviii. Parisiis, Apud Franciscum Regnault, 1535.

> The book is in octavo, both volumes bound together, both binding
> and text being in clean, excellent condition. The first 24 leaves
> of first volume, including title-page, contain a brief summary of
> the titles of the councils, an address of the engraver to the reader,

a letter from James Merlin to Stephen, Archbishop of Sens, an index of matter, an alphabetical index, followed by prefaces, &c. The rest of the volume is made up of 326 leaves, printed in double columns, with 62 lines in each column. The first 8 pages of the second volume contain a letter to the Christian reader, index of matter, and brief summary of councils. The volume contains 222 leaves in double column, 62 lines in each column. This book is rare, and is not mentioned by Panzer.

MAMMOTRECTUS, Expliciunt Expositiones et correctiones Vocabulorum Libri qui appellatus Mamotrectus tam Bibliæ quam aliorum plurimorum librorum, Impressi Venetiis per Franciscum de Hailbrun et Petrum de Bartua socios, MCCCCLXXVIII. [Hain, 10558]

Two impressions of this book appeared in 1470, both in folio: this volume is an early edition in quarto or lesser size (see Mattaire i. p. 295; Eber. iii. p. 1018). This book was put forth by a priest for the use of the less instructed in his own profession, and it is said by Santand to be compiled by John Marchesinus (see Dibdin, *Bibliotheca Spen.* vol. i. p. 157). This volume contains a brief exposition of the several books of the Old and New Testaments, including those of the Apocrypha, with short preface to each book; a short treatise of orthography and of accent; a short declaration of the months, festivals, &c. of the Jewish priests; an explanation of ancient words and terms in responses, hymns, homilies, &c.; then fol'ows a *Legenda* Sanctorum according to the order of the Breviary, and a *Commune* Sanctorum, concluding with a short Declaration of the Rules of the Minor Friars; then follows a vocabulary in alphabetical order of words used in the Mamotrectus, consisting of 25 leaves. The book is printed in double columns, 37 lines in a column; initial capitals are rubricated throughout, clean broad margin, with signatures and running title; in very good condition, and, as a MS. note states, was once the property of Robert Southey, given to him by Walter Savage Landor.

MAMMOTRECTI LIBER omnibus ecclesiasticis tam secularibus: quam religiosis summe necessarius quem Psalmorum legendarum de tempore et sanctis: insuper et Hymnorū vocabula una cū eorū quantitatibus enodat: declarat: quē novissime Petrus Viard bibliopola Parisiensis in vico divi

Jacobi sub Leone argēteo sedens, emēdatum exaratum te:-
sum politū reddidit, ad eum igitur christicole festinantes
currite qui tantum librō ere modico vobis cōdonabit. 1521.

Then follows printer's device. On the dorsal commences a vocabulary of 15 leaves in treble columns. The contents are the same
as in the other copy of the book described above, except that
this has no Commune Sanctorum, nor the declaration of the rules
of the Minor Friars.

Tome I. II.

QUESTIONES Quodlibetales ex quatuor Scntentiarum vo-
lumiuibus a Joāne duns Scoto doct. subtilissimo ordinis min
ac Theologorom pncipe editi : nuperrime, revise a preclaro doc.
Antonio de Fantis Tarvisino pristino nitori restituti : noviter-
que Impressi. Disputationes Collationales. Tabula Generalis
Scotice subtilitatis octo sectionibus universas Doctoris Subtilis
Peritias complectens ab excellentissimo doctore Antonio de
Fantis Tarvisino edita nuperrime revisa et quam plurimis
ipsis mendis purgata noviter quæ impressa. Tabula deffini-
tionum Tertia in ordine, et divisionum quarta. Sectio quinta
Scientialium Regularum ac Theorematum cui annectitur no-
tabilius Propositionum. Sectio septima Expositarum Auctori-
tatum Theologicorum ac Peripateticorum a Doctore subtili duas
in Partes distributa. Octava sectio. Tabula generalis. Printed
by Jacobus de Burgofranco, 1517.

This book is in handsome small Gothic type, in double columns,
50 lines in a column. It has engraved title-pages representing
Scotus in his study in the act of writing. It is in good condition,
handsomely bound in vellum, and gilded.

Tome III. IV.

SCRIPTUM Joanis Duns Scoti doctoris subtilis ordinis minorum super Tertio Sententiarum nuperrime ab infinitis mendis
absolutum : et ab eximio doctore Antonio de Fantis Tarvisino
pristino candori restitutum : noviter quæ impressum. Per
Jacobum Paucidrapensem de Burgofranco, 1517.

This book is printed in small handsome Gothic type, in double columns, with 50 lines in a column. It has 134 folios. On the dorso of the last folio commences a table of contents. The capitals are engraved, those commencing each section being larger than the others.

Bound up with this is

SCRIPTUM Joanis Duns Scoti doctoris subtilis ordinis minorum super Quarto Sententiarum novissime ab innumeris erroribus expurgatum.

This contains 325 folios. Printed by same printer at same time as the first part of the volume. It is in good condition, bound in vellum, and gilded. 12mo.

LAVACRUM CONSCIENTIE. [Hain, 9955]

Before the index occurs the following colophon: "Explicit Lavacrum Conscientie omnibus Sacerdotibus summe utile ac necessarium. Impressum Colonie impensis honesti viri Henrici Quentell. Anno salutis MCCCCXCIX, Die XXVIII mensis Junii." This book is intended as a kind of manual for the use of the priesthood, pointing out what ought to be their manner of life. Under the words "Lavacrum Conscientie," in large bold type, which forms the only title-page, there is a wood-engraving, representing the Infant Christ seated on an altar. Overhead is a figure of the Dove. There are figures of the Virgin and Joseph; on the other side, Zacharias and Elizabeth. At the foot is a shield, on which are three crowns in chief. Small quarto. The book is in good condition, with ample margin.

STELLA CLERICORUM. [Hain, 15077]

The rest of the title-page is a wood engraving of St. Lebuin, the patron saint of Daventer. He is standing on a tesselated floor, and is in the act of reading. Printed at Daventer, 1490. Before the colophon occur Latin verses in sixteen lines, "In laudem libelli." The colophon is, "Impressum Davetrie in platea episcopi Anno Domini 1490 vicesima quarta Decembris." The tract consists of fifteen leaves with signatures, but no pagination or name of printer. Probably by James de Breda, though the type seems older than that assigned to him in *Bibliotheca Spenceriana*. Small quarto.

EXPLANATIONES notabiles devotissimi viri Richardi Hampole eremite super lectiones illas beati Job: que solent in exequiis defunctorum legi, qui nō minus hystoriā quam tropologiam et anagogiam ad studentium utilitatem exactissime annotavit.

On the same title-page is

SERMO beati Augustini de misericordia et pia oratione pro defunctis.

Both titles are enclosed in engraved border, and also the printer's device (B. Rembolt). On the dorso of the title-page is a woodengraving representing a portion of a burial ground, and Death aiming his dart at a monk. Above the engraving are two quotations from Ecclesiasticus and Ecclesiastes, and below it is a Tetrastichon ad Lectorem. The colophon attached to Hampole's treatise states that the book was printed at Paris by Berthold Rembolt at the charge of Johannes Waterloes, 1510. Small quarto; a good specimen of printing, in good condition except a slight water-mark.

FABULARUM quæ hoc libro continentur interpretes atque authores Sunt hi Guelielmus Gondanus. Hadrianus Barlandus. Erasmus Roterodamus. Aulus Gellius. Angelus Politianus. Petrus Crinitus. Joannes Antonius Campanus. Plinius Secundas Novocomensis. Æsopi Vita ex Max Planude excerpta. In Libera Argentini apud Matthiam Schurerium.

This book is a collection of fables by Æsop and others, made by the learned Martinus Dorpius, the friend of Erasmus, for the use of the pupils of John Leup, James Papa and John Ninivita, who appear to have been eminent schoolmasters in Flanders. Printed, as appears at the end of the book, in 1516. The book is in early Roman type, small quarto. The title-page is enclosed in engraved border. This is one of the smaller works of Dorpius, and is accordingly scarce.

AURELII Augustini opuscula plurima quædam non prius impressa.

This book is in quarto, and contains thirteen tracts printed on 338 leaves, with running titles, and one leaf of register, followed by the printer's device. The colophon states that the book was printed by Dionysius Bertochi, at Venice, 1491. It is in excellent condition, in modern binding. Prefixed is a table of eight leaves, containing the subject matter of the tracts. The text is in double columns, 55 lines in each column. The capitals are rubricated, those which are initial to separate tracts being of a larger size. Toward the end of the book some of them are omitted. On the last leaf is a "Registrum Carthanum," at the end of which is the printer's device. All the early editions of Augustine's Opuscula are rare (see Clement's *Biblio. curieuse*, tome 2, p. 276, &c.).

MAILLARD.

No. 1, small 4to.

SERMONES de Adventu, May 22. Sermones Quadragesimales, July 12. Sermones Dominicales, Aug. 11. Sermones de peccati Stipendio, Aug. 22. [Hain, 10510, seqq.]

The above were all printed at Lyons in 1498, by John de Vingle.

No. 2, small 4to.

SERMONES Dominicales, Aug. 11. De Stipendio peccati, 1498, Aug. 22. Sermones de Adventu, May 22 (preached in Paris). Sermones Quadragesimales, July 12 (preached in Paris).

The above were all printed at Lyons in 1498, by John de Vingle.

No. 3, small 4to.

SERMONES Dominicales. Sermones de peccati Stipendio et Sermone de Sancta Anna, Paris, Philippus Pigouchet, 1500. Impressi Parisius per Philippum Pigouchet impensis ejus ac Johannis Petit; Johannis Richard; Durandi Gerlier: Parisiensium librariorum et Jacobi Huguetan Lugdunensis in hujusce impressione sociorum MCCCCCXIIIJ, Mense Augusti. [Hain, 10516]

No. 4, small 8vo.

SERMONES Quadragesimales (preached at Nantz). Sermones quadragesimales (preached at Bruges). Prothemata Questiones et parabolæ in premissis Sermonibus quadragesimalibus omissis.

The three are paged as forming the same volume.

Bound up with the foregoing, but differently paged, by Maillard :

SERMONES Dominicales impensis Johannis Petit Parisiensis 1506. Summarium quoddam Sermonum de Sanctis per totum Anni circulum simul et de communi Sanctorum et pro defunctis: hactenus nunquam impressorum, printed 1516. Contemplatio in S. Marie salutationem. Sermones IV in Ecclesiæ Dedicatione. Sermones VIII de Miseriis Animæ.

The several treatises, sermons, &c. were printed by John Barbier at Paris, for John Petit, 1516.

No. 5, small 8vo.

SERMONES Quadragesimales, preached at Nantz. Alia Quadragesimalium Sermonum recollectio quædam facta sub eodem verbi Dei precone ubi sicut discipulum in precedenti sic hic criminosum quemdam in medium ducit. In a note: "Intitulatum est præsens quadragesimale *Criminosi* existere eo quod in parte secunda singulorum sermonum *Criminosus* fingitur per Absolom representatus. Et primo dominica in quinquagesima mane sermonem fecit de charitate capiendo prothemate. Si charitatem non habuero nihil sum, 1 Cor. xiii. Subthema Intravit autem rex ut videret discumbentes, &c., Matth. xxii. Ibique de veste nuptiali dixit, quæ alibi in primo sermone Nanetis et questionem movit quam habes in Dominica xvi post Pentecosten et cæteraque ibidem habes propter quod quære si vis."

The contents of this volume are said to have been printed "impensis honesti viri Johannis Petit, 1513."

No. 6, small 8vo.

SERMONES Dominicales. Sermones Communes omni tempore prædicabiles. De peccati stipendio. Printed "impensis Johannis Petit Bibliopolæ, Parisiensis, 1521.

These six volumes together form a *complete* collection of the *printed* sermons, &c. of Maillard. Every volume is perfect, except a folio or two in the Quadragesimal sermons preached at Nantes; in the best condition, some on' vellum, all at least on vellum-paper, and presenting specimens of the best printing of that period. Maillard was a famous preacher in his time, and in consequence of the plain, bold language in which he reproved the vices of his day, his works are scarce. Illustrative of his character, it is related of him, that in consequence of some liberties which he took with Louis XI., king of France, who had just established a system of posting on the roads of France, one of the courtiers informed him that the king had threatened to throw him into the river; Maillard's answer was, "The king is my master, but you may tell him that I shall get sooner to heaven by water, than he will with his post-horses."

PRECORDIALISSIMI ac impreciabiles de adventu domini Sermones completi a Reverendo patre D. Joāne Cleree ordinis predicatorum generali magistro artium ac sacre pagīe doctore Parrhissiē aureo quidem ordīe editi atque declamati ad dei honorem animarumque salutem nunc primum in lucem emissi feliciter incipiunt.

Then follows the printer's device, of the pelican, &c., and the name and place of printing. There is no date. The book is in small octavo, neat Gothic type, double columns, of 46 lines each. The principal initial letters are engraved in wood. The date is probably 1522. [See Panzer viii. 80, 1337.]

DE VITA et beneficiis Salvatoris Jesu Christi devotissime Meditationes cum gratiarum actione. (12mo.)

HOROLOGIUM Devotionis circa vita Christi. (12mo.)

These two treatises are bound together, and are without name of printer or of place, having signatures but no running title. Space is left in both books for illuminated capitals, some of which have been partially supplied in the first Treatise by pen and ink. Many of the chapters in the second Treatise are headed by a wood engraving representing the subject of the chapter: to those engravings some kind of pigment seems to have been applied, and the book closed before the colour was dry. There is nothing in the præfatio of the "De Vita," &c. to indicate the author of the Treatise, but the prologue to the Horologium tells that the writer was "Frater Bertholdus sacerdos Ordinis Prædicatorum," and that he had before put forth a "Horologium" in the Teuton language, and had translated the same into Latin for the use of the learned. The two Treatises are evidently by the same printer, although the type of the "Horologium" appears to have been more worn than that of the "De Vita," &c. The book is in good condition and in the original binding.

BREVIARIUM AUREUM domini Guillelmi Duranti Speculatoris utriusque censure doctoris ac practici consummatissimi ad omnes cujusque ponderis ubilibet delitescentes materias tam glossarum quam textuum juris canonici miro operis artificio compaginatum amplectens insuper quicquid boni reconditur in preclaro fertilique apparatu Innocentie Pape quarti canonistarum facile principis ubi omnis eliminata et practicatoria Juris lucessit veritas cujus quidem operis momentanea inspectio tribuit quod annorum laboriosa multiplicitas non invenit.

Under this title is an engraving of a galley with the printer's device, underneath which is in bold letter, Galliot Du Pre. The book is in old binding (re-backed only), and is a good specimen of the printer's small Gothic type. Small octavo.

VALERIUS MAXIMUS.

Printed in Roman type. On the dorso of the title-page is a breviate of the life of Valerius Maximus, followed by a dedication of Aldus Manutius to Polonus, dated Venice, 1508, and a table of contents. The book was printed by James Marescal, at Lyons, 1513, the

device of that printer being inserted on a blank leaf immediately
preceding a "Tabula Materiarum" of 15 leaves, which, though
printed in small Gothic type, corresponds with the book in the
references to the particulars. The book is in small octavo, and
in good condition. (See Mattaire, tom. II., part I., p. 246.)

SUMMA Catholici doctoris Augustini de Ancona de potestate ecclesiastica.

This is in quarto, and the colophon states it to have been printed
at Rome "in domo nobilis viri Frācisci de Cinquinis¹ apud Sanc-
tam Mariam de populo, Anno Domini MCCCCLXXVIIII." This book
is without signature, pagination, or running title, is printed in
small, singularly neat, Gothic type, on vellum-like paper, in
double columns, 50 lines in each column.

CONSTITUTIONS PROVINCIALLES, and of Otho, and of Othobone. Translated in to Englyshe. Imprynted at London in Flete-strete by me Robert Redman, Anno M.D.XXXIIII.

The title-page is engraved, and marked with the initials I.M. This
edition is in small octavo, Gothic type, and is not commonly to
be met with.

CONSTITUTIONES Angliae Provinciales ex diversis Can-

tuariensium Archiepiscoporum Synodalibus decretis, per Guiliel-
mum Lyndewode Anglum jam olim collecte. Constitutiones
item Legatinæ, quas alii legitimas vocant, Reverendorum in
Christo patrum Othonis et Othoboni quondam sedis Apostolicæ
in Anglia legatorum nunc demum accuratius quam antehāc
alias in studiosorum gratiam impressæ. Accessit Cantuarien-
sium archiepiscoporum quorum in hoc libro Constitutiones continentur catalogus nunc primum conscriptus atque in lucem
editus. Londini, Excudebat Thomas Marshe, 1557. Sm. 8vo.

¹ "Whom the Apostolical official had made printer," *vide* Supplement to
Mattaire, page iii., number 771.

JOANNIS Stobaei Sententiāe ex Thesauris græcorum Delecta. Cyri Theodori Dialogus, de Amicitiæ Exilio. Opusculum Platoni adscriptum, de justo, Aliud ejusdem, an virtus doceri possit, Huic editioni accesserunt Ejusdem Joannis Stobæi eclogarum Physicarum et Ethicarum Libri Duo. Item Loci Communes Sententiarum collecti per Antonium et Maximum Monachos, atque ad Stobæi locis relati. Subjunctis Capitum, Auctorum, Verborum et rerum locupletessimis Indicibus. Aureliæ Allobrogum Pro Francisco Fabro, Bibliopolo Lugdunensi, M.DCIX.

Respecting this edition of Stobæus Ebert remarks, "that it is sought after, as it is the only one which contains both the works of Stobæus together." See also Dibdin's *Introduction to Greek and Latin Classics*, vol. II. The book is in folio.

SUMMA viciorum seu Tractatus moralis editus a Fratre Guilelmo episcopi Lugdunensis ordinisque fratrum prædicatore.

This book is in folio, and is an excellent specimen of early printing, and is in good preservation. It is without signature, pagination, printer's name or place. The spaces left for ornamented capitals are not filled up, except here and there, and that apparently by an amateur hand. The book has broad margins, on which occasionally appear short manuscript notes in old hand-writing. The paper-mark on the last leaf of the Capitula, and in other parts, is that found on the paper used by the first printers, viz., an ox's head with a rod proceeding out of it, terminating in a star; thus a former owner of the book has assigned the date of it to 1474—5, as printed by Berthold at Basle, and refers to Panzer i., 191, 268, whereas Berthold does not appear amongst the names of printers at Basle, but of those of Naples, and respecting whose works it may be remarked that they were very few in number.

SERMONES de Sanctis Discipuli, with the Exempla and De Miraculis Virginis. Folio. Colophon : Finit opus per utile simplicibus curam animarum gerentibus per venerabilem Johanem Herolt. Impressum Argentine Anno a Christi natali Octuagesimoquarto supra millesimum quaterque centesimum. Laus Deo. 1484.

This book has neither signatures nor printer's name, is well printed,

with a good margin. On the obverse of the first folio there is
a table and list of the Sermons: and opposite the Sermons is a
brief Registrum of the principal matter contained in the Sermons.
Then follow the *Exempla* according to the letters of the alphabet,
with a table of the matter set forth in the examples arranged
alphabetically under the respective subjects which the Exempla
were intended to set forth. The book is a specimen of very early
printing, and is in good condition, and closes with a recital of
the miracles of the Virgin, of which a table is subjoined, and
a list of the authors quoted in the Sermons. It is printed in
double columns, 49 lines in a column. The capitals are illuminated throughout. The type is very like that of John Gro-
ningen, who printed at Argentine about the date of this book.

LIBER AUREUS. Inscriptus liber conformitatum Vitæ
beatæ et seraphici Patris Francisci ad Vitam Jesu Christi
Domini nostri. Nunc denuo in lucem editus atque infinitis
propemodum mendis correctus a reverendo ac doctissimo P. F.
Jeremia Bucchio Vtinensi sodali Franciscano Doctore Theologo
laboriosis, ornatissimisque lucubrationibus illustratus. Bononiæ
apud Alexandrum Benatium. Facultate a superioribus concessa
1590.—*Edition forte-rare,* Clement, *Biblioth.*, vol. viii. pp.
448, seq. See also Eber, *Dictionar. Bibliograph.* vol. ii.
p. 937.

On the title-page is a wood engraving representing S. Francis
bearing his cross after our Lord: another in the beginning of the
first and second books representing the arm of S. Francis fastened
to the cross with that of our Lord. At the beginning of the third
book is a wood engraving representing S. Francis receiving the
five wounds. There are two former editions of this work, all of
which editions are of great rarity, and all of them stuffed full
of absurd stories, this edition less so than those preceding, in
both of which may be found the notorious story of the *spikes*
which S. Francis swallowed in the *consecrated wine.* The book
is in excellent condition, and in the original binding. Folio.

DEFENSORIUM seu Correctorium fundamentarū Doctoris
Domini Egidii Romani ordinis Eremitarum Sancti Augustini
Archiepiscopi Bituricensis in Corruptorium librorum Angelici

Doctoris sancti Thome Aquinatis ordinis prædicatorum a quodam emulo [Guillielmo de la Mare] depravatorum.

This book was printed at Venice, on vellum, 14 May, 1516, by the
heirs of Octavian Scot, a nobleman of the city of Mona, who set
up presses at Venice at his own charge, and printed a great
number of books, all of which are marked O.S.M. The type is
in a bold Gothic letter with very few contractions. In place
of illuminated capitals are well executed wood-engraved initials.
The leaves, 55 in number, are paged, and have a running title.

With this book is bound up a

FASCICULUS temporum (Wern. Rolevinck),

Which is brought down to the year 1476: is rather profusely
illustrated with well executed wood-cuts, and the leaves (64 in
number) are paged throughout, but there are no signatures. The
character of the letter is very much like that employed by the
printers of the *Defensorium* above mentioned, but not nearly so
black and used as in that book. There is no note of printer's
name or place, but taking into account that this *Fasciculus
temporum* is in general appearance, &c., like the book with which
it has been bound up, it may be most probably regarded as one
of the often repeated editions of Erhard Raldolt, printer at Venice,
somewhat earlier than Scot. Both the Defensorium and the Fasciculus are in excellent, clean condition. (See Palmer, *Hist. of
Printing*, p. 149; Eber, *Biblioth.*, ii., 558, 9.) Folio.

ENNEADES Marci Antonii Sabellici ab orbe condito Ad
inclinationem Romani Imperii. At the end of the book is the
colophon, printed in red: Impressum Venetiis per Bernardinum
et Mattheum Venetos qui vulgo dicuntur Lialbanesoti anno
Incarnationis Dominice MCCCCXCVIII pridie Calendas Aprilis,
regnante inclito Augustino Barbadico Serenissimo Venetiarum
principe. Feliciter diuque et fauste superstite diu.

The book is printed in the Roman letter, is very slightly water-
stained at the beginning, but is in general a fine folio, and good
specimen of the Venetian press. The printer's device in red follows
the colophon, and there is also a well engraved device following the
title-page on the first leaf. This is the first edition.

D. DIONYSII Carthusiani in VII Epistolas Canonicas. Jacobi, I; Petri, II; Joannis, III; Judaæ, I. Ejusdem, Acta Apostolorum, In Apocalypsim, Hymnos Ecclesiasticos. Omnia accuratius diligentiusque quam antehac recognita fuere. Apud Robertum Massellin sub trium orbium rubrorum insigni, e regione Ecclesiae divi Stephani, M.D.LI.

> Such is the title-page, but the book itself contains the commentaries of Dionysius on all the other Canonical epistles printed at Paris by Michael Fezendat in 1544. The size and quaint character of the type in both is very similar, but the volume printed by Fezandat is in the newer type. Both are good specimens of the French printing, more particularly the wood-engraved capitals, those of Fezandat being the clearer and more elaborately executed.

SACRE Theologie Magistri necnon sacri eloquii præconis celeberrimi fratris Roberti Episcopi Acquino ordinis minorum processoris opus quadragesimale perutilissimumque quod de penitentia doctum est.

> The colophon, after reciting the title,[1] adds: "Venetiis impressum est impensis Johannis de Colonia: ac socii ejus Johannis Manthen de Gherretzen, M.CCCC.LXXVI." The book is in quarto, printed in a small, elegant, Gothic type, in two columns, with signatures, no running titles; clean, in good condition, and with wide margins. Blank spaces left for illuminated capitals, supplied by small letters.

BAPTISTÆ Fulgosi de dictis factisque memorabilibus collectaneata Camillo Gilino Catina facta.

> In a long colophon it is stated among other things that the work was originally written in Italian by Fulgose (or Fregose) and translated into Latin by Camillus Gilinus, and that it was printed at Milan in 1509, by Jacobus Ferrarius. On the dorso of the title-page (as recited above) is the letter of Camillus Gilinus to Charles VIII., king of France: this is followed by Fulgosius' address to his son Peter, concluding with a list of the authors

---

[1] Adding, "cum ceteris tribus sermonibus ci annexis."

from whom his collection of anecdotes was derived. This collection, professedly after the names of Valerius Maximus, is comprised in nine books, of each of which a table of contents is given. Ebert says in his *Bibliograph. Dict.*, vol. ii., p. 611, "This original edition is scarce and prized : there is a copy on vellum in the Royal Library at Paris. The editions of Paris, 1518, 4to; Ant., 1565, 8vo; Col., 1604, 8vo, are inferior." The book is in folio, printed in good, bold type, with broad margin, bound in vellum.

BEATI Joannis Damasceni orthodoxæ fidei accurata Explicatio.

Printed in Greek and Latin, parallel columns, Basileæ per Henrichum Petri, 1548, with his device on the title-page. On the dorso of the title-page is a list of all the treatises contained in this volume.

Bound in the same volume is

PHILIPPI Presbyteri viri longe eruditissimi in Historiam Job Commentariorum. Basileæ per Adamum Petrum mense Augusto, M.D.XXVII.

The whole volume is a good specimen of Greek and Latin type, with a good margin, and in the original binding. Folio.

SPECULUM Exemplorum (sive Libri exemplorum) ex diversis libris in unum laboriose collectum.

The colophon informs us that this collection of examples was made by Richard Paefroed, a citizen of Daventer, and printed by him on the morrow of S. Philip and S. James' day, 1481. Prefixed to the book is an alphabetical table of the general matters contained in the book, containing 39 leaves of 40 lines each. The matter of the book is divided into ten distinctions or divisions, and consists of extracts or anecdotes derived from various sources, those sources being severally described at the commencement of each distinction. The text is in a clear Gothic type, arranged in double columns, 40 lines each, broad margin, and is among the first books that issued from Paefroed's press. The book is in old monastic binding, and in very good condition, except the last two leaves, which have been injured by the damp.

HISTORICA Longobardica. Explicit Historia Longobardica diligenter impressa ac correcta cum nonnullis Sanctorum et Sanctarum legendis in fine superadditis per me Conradum Winters de Hamburch Coloniæ civem Anno Dni. M.CCCCLXXX.

In a copy mentioned by Mattaire (*Ann. Typ.*, tom. I., par. 1, Amsterdam, 1733) there is added to the colophon above written, "et per me Conradum Dusseldorf rubricum." The description of the book thus rubricated is "*Splendidum et illuminatum exemplar.*" Now the copy in my possession may be truly described as a "*splendidum* exemplar"; but the only rubrication in it is the supply of all the initial letters by hand in *red* ink. The texture of the paper may, moreover, vie in substance and appearance with vellum, and the book is in original monastic binding, in good condition, in Gothic letters, with signatures and tabula, but no running title. Double columns, 40 lines in a column, 363 leaves.

AUCTORES Historiæ Ecclesiasticæ Eusebii Pamphili Cæsariensis Episcopi libri ix. Ruffino interprete. Ruffini Presbyteri Aquileiensis libri ii. Item, Theodorito Episcopo Cyrensi Sozomeno et Socrate Constantinopolitano, libri xii. versi ab Epiphanio Scholastico abbreviati per Cassiodorum Senatorem: unde illis Tripartitæ historiæ vocabulum. Omnia recognita ad antiqua exemplaria Latina per Beatum Rhenanum. His accesserunt Nicephori Ecclesiastica Historia incerto interprete. Victoris Episcopi libri iii. de persecutione Wandalica. Theodoriti libri v. nuper ab Joachimo Camerario latinitate donati. Basileæ XLIIII., 1544.

Printed by Frobenius and Nicolaus Episcopius, with the device of Frobenius on title. A splendid example of early printing, and a signally fine volume. Folio.

PROCOPII Cæsariensis de Rebus Gothorum Persarum ac Vandalorum libri vii. una cum aliis mediorum temporum historicis quorum catalogum sequens indicabit pagina. His omnibus accessit rerum copiosissimus index. Basiliæ ex officina Joannis Hervagii mense Septembri Anno M.D.XXXI. Folio.

The title-page has the printer's device, and the initial capital letters are highly ornamented wood engravings; the book has good margins, and is in clean and good condition; a fine specimen of early printing.

ALFONSI a Castro, Zamorensis, Ordinis Minorum regularis Observantiæ: Provinciæ S. Jacobi adversus omnes Hæreses libri xiiii. Antverpiæ, In ædibus Joannis Steelsii anno M.D.LVI.

The royal arms of Spain are engraved on the title-page. The book is in good condition, and is an excellent example of Stelsius' printing. Folio.

CONCORDANTIE majores biblie tam dictionum declinabilium quam indeclinabilium de novo summa diligentia cum textu vise ac secundum veram ortographiam emendatissime excuse. Colophon at the end of first part as follows : " Concordantie dictionum declinabilium totius biblie opera et impensis Johannium Amorbachii, Petri de Langendorff, et Frobenii de Hammelburg jam denuo in urbe Basileo felici consummatione finiunt. Anno gratiæ millesimo supra quingentesimum sexto pridie kalendis Marcii." Colophon at the end of second part as follows : " Concordantie Biblie partium sive dictionum in declinabilium a prestantissimo viro magistro Johanne de secubia sacre pagine doctore eximio in concilio Basiliensi edite: impresseque per Joannes Amorbachium Petri et Frobenium. Anno domini Milesimo quingentessimo sexto tertia decima die mensis Martii expliciunt."

At the back of the title-page is a preface by F. Conrad Leontorius, a Cistercian monk of Mulbronnen, dated 1506. The book is printed in small dark type, in three columns, somewhat wormed, but not interfering with the text. Folio, in good condition, with good margin; a minute verbal concordance of the whole Vulgate text.

BEATI Rhenani Selestadiensis Rerum Germanicarum libri tres ab ipso Autore diligenter revisi et emendati addito memora-

bilium rerum Indice accuratissimo. Quibus præmissa est Vita
beati Rhenani Joanne Sturmio eleganter conscripta.
Printed by Froben. Basileæ, 1551 (beautifully printed).

In the same volume.

DE GERMANORUM prima Origine Moribus Institutis Legibus et memorabilibus pace et bello gestis omnibus omnium
seculorum usque ad Mensem Augustum Anni trigessimi
noni supra millessimum quingentesimum libri Chronici xxxi.
ex probatioribus Germanicis Scriptoribus in Latinam linguam
translati autore H. Mutio.
Printed Basileæ apud Henricum Petrum.

In the same volume.

CHRONOGRAPHIA Ecclesiæ Christianæ qua dilucide Patrum et Doctorum Excellentium ordo cum omnium Haeresum
origine et multiplici innovatione Decretorum et Ritum in Ecclesia per Imperatores, Principes, Concilia, aut Pontifices Romanos
a Christi nativitate ad nostra tempora usque ostenditur Ad
S. Patrum Lectionem rerumque ecclesiasticarum cognitionem
utilis et necessaria. Principio industria ac labore Henrici Pan-
taleonis Basiliensis in gratiam studiosorum veritatis ex His-
toricorum Patrum et Chronicorum monumentis concinnatu.
Nunc vero ab eodem diligentissime revisa, locupletata atque
denuo in lucem ædita. Basileæ, apud Nicolaum Brylingerum,
mense Augusti, Anno M.D.LI.
All good specimens of the works of the several printers, the title-
pages in each volume bearing the devices of the several printers.

Besides the foregoing three works the same volume contains:

CATALOGUS Annorum et principum sive Monarcharum
Mundi Geminus plerisque in locis obscurioribus illustratus
&c. Cum accessione multorum aliorum quæ in priori editione
non continebantur quemadmodum suis locis toti libro videre
licebit ab Homine condito, usque in præsentem, a nato Christi
millessimum quingentessimum et quinquagessimum annum

deductus et continuatus per D. Valerium Anselmum. Ryd.
Ex magnifica Helvetiorum urbe Berna Anno Domini M.D.L.

This book is illustrated by many woodcuts representing the his-
torical events and persons of the world. On one or more of the
engravings occur the initials I.K., probably those of James
Kerver, a wood engraver of Frankfort, of about A.D. 1540, who is
spoken of in Bryan's *Dict. of Painters and Engravers* (vol. i.,
p. 597) as having published a set of cuts of grotesque figures, &c.
for a folio volume entitled " Catalogus Annorum." A comparison
of this volume with Conrad Lycosthenis' Prodigiorum Chronicon,
printed at Basle about the same date, might perhaps shew that the
wood engraving in both books proceeded from the same hand.
The printer's name is not given.

CATALOGUS Sanctorum ex diversis ac doctis voluminibus
congestus a Reverendissimo in Christo patre domino Petro de
Natalibus de Venetiis, Dei gratia Episcopo Equilino ac jam
denuo accurate revisus. Anno M.D.XXI.

This title is inserted on a very well executed engraved title-page,
at the bottom of which is a blank shield, on which are written
H.R.W., the initials apparently of a former owner of the book,
with the date 1562. I do not find any printer's name or place.
N.B. The intial letters for the first few folios are elaborate wood
engravings, afterwards plain, bold Roman capitals, but in several
instances the initial place is blank. The book is in small, clean,
Gothic type, with very few contractions, and in the original
binding, with clasps. Folio.

TRACTATUS imprescripti venerabilis magistri Hugonis de
sancto victore: viz., De sacramentis; Didascalon; De anima
christi; De laude charitatis; Quo studio orandus fit Deus;
Mysterium de filia Jepte; Notule super quosdam psalmiste
versus. Sententie vel assertiones in quibusdam verbis divinis
et rerum naturis. De judicio veri et boni. Epistola Ugonis
ad Joannem hyspalensem Archiepiscopum. The colophon
states: Venetiis accuratissime in mandato et expensis domini
Benedicti fontanæ. Per Jacobum pentium Leucensem. 1506.

A table of contents precedes each of the two books on the Sacraments,
and at the end of the whole book is a table referring to the Notule

and the Sententie, followed by the colophon. Below this are the register of signatures, and the double-headed black eagle of the Roman empire on a globe enclosed in a border, which may be taken for the printer's device. The book is in Roman type, 191 leaves, double columns. Many of the principal chapters have an elaborately engraved initial letter. Folio. Bound in vellum.

LE VITE de sancti padri per diversi eloquentissimi doctori vulgarizate. Colophon: Explicit vita sanctorum patrum Hermannus lichtenstein coloniensis probatissimus librarie artis exactor. Impressum Vincentie anno domini, 1479.

> The book is in folio, old monastic Italian binding. It is printed in neat, small Gothic type, broad margins, double columns, each containing 60 lines. The following leaves are wanting, sig. A 1, B 2, last blank of I, K 1, K 3. In other respects the book is perfect, in good clean condition. Lichtenstein was one of the first to introduce printing into Vincentia, though he was of unsettled habit, being found among the printers of Treviso and Venice. Palmer's *Hist. of Print.*, p. 229. Folio.

RATORUM omnium Poetarum: Hystoricorum: ac Philosophorum eleganter dicta; per Clarissimum virum Albertum de Eyb in unum collecta feliciter Incipiunt. The colophon is as follows: Summa Oratorum omnium: Poetarum: Hystoricorum: ac Philosophorum Autoritates in unum collecte per Clarissimum virum Albertum de Eyb Utriusque Juris doctorem eximium: que Margarita poetica dicitur: feliciter finem adepta est. A.D. 1480.

> This book is a commonplace book of elegant extracts from many authors, and must have been popular at the time, since there were several editions of it printed in the fifteenth century in different countries. Dibdin (*Biblioth. Spen.*, vol. iii., p. 313), quotes from Bunneman, who says "that the work abounds with various erudition, and is justly held in estimation by many," &c. The book is without name of printer or place, there are no signatures, but each leaf (242 in all, besides those of the table) is numbered by Roman numerals. The table of contents at the beginning

occupies twelve leaves, followed by one blank leaf. The work commences with the author's dedication to John, Bishop of Munster. The initial letter, and top and bottom of the first page being ornamented by gilded illuminations, it may be conjectured that this copy was intended for the Bishop of Munster himself.

ISIDORI Etymologiarum opus Idem de summo bono.

The two treatises contained in this book are without date or name of printer or place, but were evidently printed conjointly at the end of the fifteenth or early in the sixteenth century. The book is in small, neat Gothic type, very like that employed by Octavian Scot, of Venice, and his partners, and is printed in double columns of 65 lines each, with broad margins, on strong vellum-like paper. Each treatise has its distinct pagination and signatures. The whole of the dorso of page 35 in lib. 9 of the Etymologiarum is occupied by an "Arbor Consanguinitatis." At the end of each treatise is a table of its contents. The initial letters of the chapters are engraved throughout the book. The volume is in good clean condition and in the original parchment cover.

SERMONES Funebres, necnon Nuptiales, tam communes, quam particulares, in quacunque materia ad quotidianos usus aptissimi, etc.

Below this title is an engraved device and a note directing the reader to the dorso of the title-page for the contents of the book. These sermons were collected by Gregory, an English Dominican monk (see Pitsius, p. 844), and seem to have been often reprinted. This edition, the colophon informs us, was printed at Venice in 1540, by Rabanus and his partners. The book is printed in Gothic type, in double columns, with running titles, pagination and signatures, small octavo, and modern binding.

OPERA Johannis Gersonis Cancellarii Parisiensis. In 3 parts, small 4to. The colophon at the end of the first part is: Prima pars, complectens tractatus fidem ac potestatem ecclesiasticam concernentes, finit feliciter. Anno Dom. 1489, mense vero, Dec. x. kal. At the end of the second part: Secunda pars, continens Opuscula ad mores accommodata. Explicit feliciter, Anno salutis 1489, Quinto nonas Aug. At the end of the third part: Finiunt opera Cancellarii Parisiensis, Anno Dom.'1489, xii kal. mensis Novembris.

All the parts are in good, plain Gothic type, in double columns, 50 lines in each column; have signatures, pagination, and running titles, but are without printer's name or place. Gesner, in his *Bibliot. Instit.* (sub. nom. "Gerson"), states that there was an edition in 1488 at Argentine, but gives no printer's name. It is not improbable that this edition was printed at the same place, and that by Martin Flack, who occasionally withheld his name. For description of this edition see Supp. ad Maittaire, pars. 1, p. 286. The first two parts are handsomely bound, the third is in plain vellum.

LIBER eruditionis religiosorum : in quo quicquid preclarum et utile in aliis religiosorum instructionibus continetur: hic ingeniose connucleatum, atque solerti cura collectum invenies, et hunc compilavit magister Humbertus de Romanis quondam generalis ordinis predicatorum : quem noviter correxerunt et impressioni tradiderunt patres ordinis minorum conventus Parisiensis reformatores. Venalis reperitur in vico collegii Belvacensis in officina Henrici Stephani e regione schole Decretorum.

The date is given in the colophon, 1512. This is a kind of manual for those who entered the monastic life, giving them sundry directions for their conduct and suggesting many considerations for their spiritual benefit. It may be presumed to have been a popular manual among the monastic orders (though very little known by bibliographers), since—though drawn up by Humbertus de Romanis, General of the Dominicans—this edition was put forth for the use of the Franciscans. Appended to the manual are, "Contemplatio super vita Christi," by St. Anselm; "Ordinem Vite religiose," by Bonaventura; and "Preparatio ad Missam," in the form of ejaculatory prayers taken from the Psalms. The book is in small octavo, clear Gothic type, in single column and with good clean margins.

SERMONES quadragesimales de peregrinatione generis humani a venerabili patre fratre Johanne Reynardi, etc.

The printer's device on the title-page. In the same volume are printed the same author's quadragesimal sermons "De infirmitatibus generis humani." Both series are printed by Stephen Baland at Lyons, in 1515, and are in Gothic type, double columns, with good margins. The book is in old binding, and a fair specimen of the Lyons press.

SERMONES de Adventu tam Dominicales quam feriales. A reverendo patre domino Johanne Clerce ordinis predicatorum Generali Magistro artium ac sacre pagine Doctore Parrhisiensis. Ibidem declamati. Rursusque emaculati, ac denuo circiter tempus ipsum adventus, Impressi 1529. Venundantur Parrhisiis, in via ad divum Jacobum sub signo Pellicani: ab Engleberto marnesio Bibliopola jurato. Ad edem divi Ivonis cōmorante. Pariter et ejusdem quadragesimale.

JACOBI Lathomi Theologiæ Professoris apud Lovavienses, duæ Epistolæ: una in libellum de Ecclesia, Phillippo Melanchthoni inscriptum: altera contra orationem factiosorum in Comitiis Ratisbonensis habitam. Veneunt Antverpiæ Gregorio Bontio, sub scuto Basiliensi super pontem cameræ. 1544.

HOMELIE Divi Haymonis, Episcopi Halberstattensis, in Evangelia Dominicalia, etc. Quibus adjecimus decem Homelias. Printed at Paris by Anthony Bonnemere, 1531.

Besides a table of the Homilies at the beginning, there is an alphabetical index at the close. The book is in small octavo, Roman type. It was once the property of Hen. VIII., whose Arms are impressed on the binding.

BEATI Vincentii, etc. Sermones Hycmales.

The volume was edited, with marginal notes, by Damianus Diaz.
Printed at Antwerp by the widow and heirs of Stelsius, 1572.
In Roman type, small octavo.

RADULPHI Ardentis Pictavi, Doctoris Theologi Perantiqui,
Illustrissimi Aquitaniæ Ducis Guilielmi hujus nominis quarti,
Concionatoris disertissimi in Epistolas et Evangelia (ut vocant)
Sanctorum, Homiliæ, etc.

Then follows the device of the publisher, widow of John Stelsius.
The printer was Theodore Lyndane, Antwerp, 1573. The book is
in small, neat Roman type, of one column, octavo. Radulphus
Ardens (or Raoul L'Ardent) lived early in the 12th century, and
was a somewhat voluminous writer, but it does not appear that
any carly editions of his works were printed. This edition of
Antwerp, 1573, is not mentioned by the usual bibliographers.

MARSILIUS Ficinus Florentinus de triplici vita.

This book is in octavo, bold Roman type, one of the earlier editions,
having on the title-page the device of George Wolf, who printed
at Paris between 1491 and 1499. The book is in modern binding,
but in good condition.

PRAGMATICA Sanctio cum repertorio noviter egregie desuper
compilato: ad materias facilius inveniendas: unacum tabula
alphabetica. The colophon is as follows: Finiunt decreta Ba-
siliensia necnon Bituricensia: que Pragmatica sanctio intitu-
lantur: glossata per magistrum Cosmam Guymier utriusque
juris licentiatum. Una cum repertorio sequenti noviter per
ordinem alphabeti desuper compilato. per Petrum cambasore
incentiatum in decret. Impressaque Lugduni partium francie
amenissima urbe: per Johannem de Vingle artis impressorie
magistrum. 1499.

The Pragmatic Sanction, and the Commentary upon it by the eminent lawyer mentioned in the colophon, contains in substance the Decrees of the Council of Basle, and was agreed upon at the council of bishops and clergy of France summoned at Bourges by King Charles VII. of France, by way of checking the encroachments of the Papal power on the liberties of the Gallican Church. The book is one of the earliest, if not the first edition of that famous document. It is printed in Gothic type, with an engraving on the second leaf of King Charles sitting in council, the Commentary being in double columns, divided by rubricated lines, and the text in larger type. The volume closes with a table of catchwords on two leaves; on the dorso of the last leaf is the printer's device. The book is in old binding, with gilt edges, and in good condition, and has "blooming capitals," as is usual in books printed by Vingle. Small octavo.

VITE ducentorum et triginta summorum pontificum: a beato Petro apostolo usque ad Julium secundum modernum Pontificem.

Below this title is a representation of the Pope seated. The colophon states that the book was printed at Basle by James de Pfortzheim, 1507, probably the first edition, as the history it contains is brought down to 1503. Under the title of John VIII. an account is given of the female Pope, Joan.

EVAGATORIUM Optimus Modus predicandi. Sermones XIII. Michaelis de Hungaria universales cum applicationibus Thematum perutilibus, de Tempore et de Sanctis: omni tempore predicabiles. Sermones electissimi de Rosario Beate Virginis Marie. Et de sancta Anna ejus matre. Passio Domini Nostri Jesu Christi, cum sermone ejusdem post cenam habito, ex quattuor evangelistis diligentissime collecta.

The colophon states that the contents of the book were collected by Jacobus Gaudensis, and printed at Cologne by Quentel, 1505. The book is in Gothic type, single columns, in original binding, small octavo.

SERMONES Dominicales per totum annum (cum suis concordantiis veteris et novi testamenti jurisque canonici i marginibus i ferte) per Anthonium de Bitonto ordinis fratrum minorem de observantia.

> The colophon states that the book was printed by John Groninger, Strasburg. It is in octavo, printed in small Gothic type, in double columns, 36 lines in each column. It has signatures, pagination and running titles; the paging is irregular, but according to the signatures the book is perfect, having moreover a duplicate of the first sermon. Anthonius was Bishop of Bitello, and transferred to the bishopric of Bitonto by Boniface IX. in 1399 (vide *Bibliot. Sacrée*).

HISTORIA Scholastica, by Petrus Comestor.   Quarto.

> The book consists of 303 leaves, the text being in double columns, each column containing 42 lines, with rubricated capitals. The book is in monastic binding, and in clean excellent condition, but without signatures, pagination, printer's name, place or date. Two leaves are supplied in manuscript exactly corresponding in type and paper with the rest of the book, the one connected with the book of Deuteronomy, the other with that of Joshua. There is a blank leaf at the end of the book of Joshua. The type is in many respects like that of Conrad de Winters, who did not always supply place or date.

CONFESSIONALE seu Interrogatorium Reverendi patris fratris Jacobi philippi (Bergomensis) noviter editum. Colophon: Impressum Antwerpie juxta portam camere per me Henricii eckert de hornberch.   Anno domini 1507.

> On the dorso of the title-page occurs the dedication of James Philip to John Maria, of Venice, General of the Canons Regular of San Salvador. Then follows a table of the subjects of interrogation by the confessor, and next the "Persuasio" of the writer to a certain confessor. The rest of the book contains the subjects for interrogation, comprehending, as is usual in such manuals, the indication of all possible sins. The book is in Gothic type, small octavo, and in good condition, except that a few leaves are stained in the lower margins.

56

INTRODUCTORIUM confessorum Fratris Hieronymi Savon-
arole Ferrariensis ordinis predicatorum. Venundantur ab
Joanne parvo Henrico Jacobi et Ascensio. Colophon: Finem
cepit in edibus Ascensianis ad xiiii Calendas Martias. Anno
MD.x calculum Romanum.

Savanorola, after giving his reasons for drawing up the Manual,
treats principally of offences against the Decalogue, but does not
enter into the minute details of crimes against the law of God
which are found in most manuals of this description. The book
contains 56 leaves, is in small octavo, Gothic type, single columns
of 31 lines each. As a specimen of typography it may be regarded
as worthy of notice as being printed by Jodocus Badius, when in
partnership with John Petit and Henry James at Paris. For it
will be remembered that Badius originally printed at Lyons, and
is said to have removed to Paris about the year 1500, with the
design of substituting the Roman type for the Gothic, and he
there established an excellent printing office under the name of
Prælum Ascensianum (see Palmer's *Hist. Print.* pp. 176, 234, 235;
Chalmer's *Biog. Dict.* "Badius").

LIBELLUS de modo penitendi et confitendi. The rest of the
title-page is occupied by an elaborately engraved device surrounded by the following motto: "Alaventure tout vient Apoint
qui peut Atendre." Denis Roce. Colophon: Liber de modo
penitendi et confitendi explicit feliciter. Impressus Parisiis
per Guillermus anabat Impensis Godefrido de marnef.

On the dorso of the last page is Marnet's device of the pelican, etc.
The book is in Gothic type.

ENCHIRIDION Confessariorum seu Praxis Fori Pænitentialis,
in Casibus extra et Ordinariis, etc. Accedunt in Appendice
Extractus Canonum Pænitentialium; Casus reservati; Pro-
positiones in hac materia proscriptæ; et alia quædam tam Con-
fessariis, quam Poenitentibus scitu necessaria. Authore R. P.
Joanne Townson Anglo-Benedictino ex Lambspring. Printed
at Hildesheim by J. L. Schlegel, 1705.

The book is dedicated to the Bishop of Hildesheim, and is in three parts, each containing several chapters: part 1st, De Prærequisitis, etc.; part 2nd, De Actuali Administratione, etc.; part 3rd, De Officio, etc. The book is in small octavo, Roman type, bound in vellum, and probably formed a manual for English priests.

TRACTATUS brevis et utilis pro infirmis visitandis et confessionem eorum audiendis.

This manual for confessors consists of six leaves, small quarto; it has neither signatures, pagination, date nor name of printer or place, but is evidently a specimen of early printing (circa 1470). The early handbooks for the Confessional are scarce and very little known, on account of their having been intended only for the use of the clergy: they are thus but seldom bibliographically described.

NICHOLAS de Lyra in Testamentum vetus.

This is the first volume of the edition printed in four volumes at Venice by John de Cologne, Nicholas Jenson et Socii, 1481. The additions to Lyra are by Paul Burgensis, and the replication by Matthew Doring (see Long's *Bibliot. Sac.* p. 252, Paris, 1723, and *Bibliot. Sussex*, vol. I., part 2, p. 342). The book is imperfect at the beginning, is somewhat water-stained in parts, but is otherwise in good condition, with fine broad margin. The type is similar to that used by the same printers in the book, " Summa de Casibus Asterianus," but looks somewhat more wormed. It is in original binding. Folio.

OPERA B. Fulgentii Aphri, Episcopi Ruspensis, Theologi antiqui. Nuper in vetustissimo codice apud Germanos inuenta, obsoletis et Longobardicis literis conscripta. Antea nunquam impressa. Nunc primum, ad rectiorem veteris Theologie institutionem, qua ut eruditione intellectus, sic lingua eloquio et vita moribus cultior fiat, Deo auspice, pro desyderiis votisquæ multorum in lucem emissa. Item opera Maxentii Johannis, servi Dei, pulchra vetustatis Monumenta, in eodem Codice reperta. Folio. The Colophon: Expliciunt opera B. Fulgentii

Episcopi, et Maxentii servi Dei. Impressa in Hagenau, impensis Kobergerorum Norinbergensium. In officina Thomae Anshelmi. Anno xx (1520).

This seems to be the *first* edition of Fulgentius and Maxentius, and different from that printed in Hagenau in 1520 (see Ebert *Bibliograph. Dict.*, vol. II., p. 611). The title-page, both of the works of Fulgentius and those of Maxentius, is engraved, and the book is a good specimen of early printing, in good condition, except having the margin of some leaves slightly wormed. It is scarce.

OPUS trivium validis auctoritatibus tam ex lege divina: canonica: quam civili refertissimum cunctisque verbi dei declamatoribus perquam necessarium. The following is the colophon: Opus trivium a venerabili viro. F. Johanne de Bromyard ordinis predicatorum doctore theologo nationis anglice editum. Castigatum vero per F. Symonē Bertherii ejusdem ordinis sacre theologie professorem bene meritum expensis probi viri magistri Johānis Jenini alias dyamantier explicitum est. Impressus vero arte et industria Nicolai Wolff alemani, anno christiane salutis 1500.

The book is a collection of ecclesiastical and other terms arranged alphabetically. The following sentence at the beginning of the book gives the reason for the title of *Trivium :* " Incipit trivium secundum ordinem alphabeti. Et dicitur trivium quia triplici distinctione utitur in quolibet vocabulo : etiam quia a tribus legibus divina canonica et civili capit testimonium."

ONUS Ecclesiae temporibus hisce deplorandis Apocalypseos suis æque conveniens, Turcarumque incursui jam grassanti accommodatum, non tam lectu quam contemplatu dignissimum : jam primum autoris exactiore adhibita lima typis a mendosis expurgatum ; et quam plurimis tum Evangelistarum locis tum aliorum Sanctorum scripturis mutuo non pugnantibus, recens illustratum. 1531.

From the colophon it appears that this book was written in 1519, and was no doubt circulated in MS. though not printed till 1531. This is therefore the first and very scarce edition of a work which attracted great attention at the time; the names of the printer, and of the place where it was printed are not given. The *Onus Ecclesiæ* was printed in 1535 in a collection of similar treatises known as "Fasciculus rerum expetendarum," etc.; and Gesner also mentions a separate edition printed at Cologne in 1583. The title is enclosed in a curiously engraved border, containing several texts of Scripture describing the judgments threatened by the prophets and our Lord to the Jewish nation; under each text is an engraved representation of the judgment referred to. On the dorso of the title-page is a singular engraving, at the base of which is represented a church which the evil spirit is attempting to destroy by fire and sword; overhead are the apocalyptic angels uttering their threats or pouring out their vials upon the earth. The book is printed in clear, bold Gothic type, in double columns, 50 lines in a column. After the prologue is a table of the contents of the book, and at the end of the book is an alphabetical index of the subjects. It is in modern binding, and is in clean excellent condition.

DOCTORIS Joannis Fabri, adversus Doctorem Balthasarum Pacimontanum Anabaptistarum nostri saeculi, Primum authorem orthodoxae Fidei Catholica defensio. Then follows Exekiel xiii. 3—10, printed at length from the Latin Bible; after which is: Gratia, auctoritate, privilegioque cũ Sereniss. Vngarie Bohemieque Regis Ferdinãdi, tũ Caesareæ Maiesta. Melchior Lotther hoc opus percudit, in hoc, ne quis ad decenniũ usquæ, sub, decẽ marcarũ auri, puri, mulcta, ĩprimat.

The colophon states that the book was printed at Leipsic by Melchior Lotther in 1528. It is in fine bold type, and is an excellent specimen of the early press of Leipsic; in good condition, and monastic binding. Scarce, small quarto.

REPLIQUE pour le Catholique Anglois contre le Catholique associé des Huguenots. M.D.LXXXVIII.

The title-page bears a woodcut, representing the Virgin Mary and St. John standing by the cross of our Lord. This tract, which contains 23 duodecimo leaves, is of extreme rarity, being one of those brochures which the Duke of Guise, when at the head of the League in France, caused to be surreptitiously circulated in

France, for the purpose of preventing Henry, the Protestant king of Navarre, from succeeding to the throne of France. To accomplish that object, the duke employed Louis d'Orleans, a profligate French attorney, to write a pamphlet under the name of "An English Catholic exile," in which he endeavoured to alarm the French nation by a false recital of the cruelties which a Protestant king, after the example of queen Elizabeth of England, would be sure to inflict on all his Protestant subjects. Although the false statements of "An English Catholic" were exposed by the Huguenots, the effect of it and other writings of a like nature was so great that the king of France was compelled to rescind an edict which had a few years before been promulgated in favour of the Huguenots, and thus left them to the mercy of the League (see Laval's *History of the Reformation in France*, vol. IV., pp. 413, etc., etc., London, 1740).

DE HAERETICIS, an sint persequendi et omnino quomodo sit cum eis agendum, Luteri et Brentii, aliorumque: multorum tum ueterum tum recentiorum sententiæ. Liber hoc tam turbulento tempore pernecessarius, et cum omnibus, tum potissimum principibus et magistratibus utilissimus, ad discendum, quod nam sit eorum in re tam controuersa, tam que periculosa, officium. Quæ nam hic contineantur, proxima pagella monstrabit. Is qui secundum carnem natus erat, persequebatur eum qui natus erat secundum spiritum, Gal. 4.

This book, though published anonymously, is ascribed to Sebastianus Castalio, who, though professedly amongst the reformers of the sixteenth century, is said to have maintained many heterodox opinions. The volume is considered very rare. At the end of the book occurs "Magdeburgi, per Georgium Rausch, Anno Domini 1554, Mense Martio." Bound up with the book is a manuscript copy of the convention between Pius VII. and the French Republic during the first Consulate.

GUILLERMUS Parisiensis. De septem sacramentis.

On the title-page is the device of the printer, Jaques le forestier. Two animals, apparently lions, supporting a shield which leans against a tree; the name of the printer below. The shield bears a Paschal Lamb with three fleur de lis in chief. The whole device

is enclosed in an ornamental border. The book is in 12mo, printed
in Gothic type, but without date, though most probably of the
early part of the sixteenth century.

The same volume contains

GUILLERMUS episcopus parisiensis de collationibus et plura-
litate ecclesiasticorum beneficiorum. Then follows the printer's
device, his name being introduced. The following is the
colophon: Finit Guillermus parisiensis decollationibus et plu-
ralitate ecclesiasticorum beneficiorum. Impressus parisius impensis Gaufridi de Marnet commorantis invico divi Jacobi sub
intersignio pelicani. Anno domini Millesimo quinquagesimo
quinto, Die vero, xxiii. Mensis Maii.

The volume is in the original parchment binding and in good
condition.

POSTILLA Majores super Evangelia et Epistolas quemadmodum in Templis per annum leguntur; non minus utiles
quam familiares [by William Paris if not William of Paris,
vide Dupin *Biblioth.* fourteenth century].

MONOTESSARON Passionis Christi ex quatuor Evangelistis
confectum et expositum diligenter per autores receptos. Index
sententiarum et dictionum in calce additus. Colophon to the
Postilla: Postillæ majores in Epistolas et Evangelia, industria
ac impensa viri Adæ Petri de Langendorff, caleographiæ
gnari exaratæ nuper ex propria officina urbis Basileæ Anno legis
gratiæ Millessimo quingentissimo decimonono Mensis vero
Februarii, die vicessima quarta. Finiunt felicitur. Colophon to
the *Monotessaron:* Explicit concordantia quatuor Evangelistarum in Passionem Domini nostri Jesu Christi inter priscas haud
facile secedet secunda in Fratre Daniele Agricola observantino
ordinis Minorum concinne digestas Operaque Adæ Petri de
Langendorff accuratissime ære plano, lucidoque distincte notulis

variis et punctuatim, mense Februarii, Basileæ, impressa,
Regnante Domino nostro Jesu Christo Anno MDXIX, Cui laus
et gloria per infinita sæcula seculorum. Amen.

This book has an elaborately engraved title-page, with the cypher
of the artist (Van Goar) at the foot of it. On the reverse of the
prologue is an engraving crowded with the figures of the four
Evangelists, St. Paul, and others. A facsimile of the engraved
title-page and crowded engraving of the Evangelists occurs at the
commencement of the Monetessaron, whilst each of the Postillas
on the Evangelists is introduced by a wood engraving representing
the subjects to which the several Gospels refer, e.g. the Postilla
for the first Sunday in Advent is headed by a wood engraving
representing the triumphal entry of our Lord into Jerusalem
(S. Matt. xxi.), and so of the remaining Postillas. Every act in
the Monotessaron Passionis Christi is introduced by a wood engraving representing the act of suffering that is recorded. Many
of the engravings have the cypher of the engraver on them, and
all of them display great freedom and distinctness in the execution.
The book itself is well printed, is in good condition, and in the old
binding. Sm. 4to. Van Goar chiefly engraved frontispieces and book
ornaments, yet his engravings are executed with so much spirit
and in so masterly a style that his prints are much esteemed (see
Bryan, *Dict. of Painters and Engravers*, " Goar").

PRODIGNORUM ac Ostentorum Chronicon per Conradum
Lycosthenem, Basileæ per Henricum Petrum, 1557.

The book is full of representations of monstrosities in the human
body, and in nature, far more extravagant than the Siamese twins.
Many of the wood-cuts are engraved, but a good many of them
are said to have been borrowed from books published by Fros-
cheverut Zurch, some from Brunster's *Cosmographia* and other
works published in Germany and Switzerland (see *The Bookworm*,
vol. I., pp. 71, etc., new series). The wood-cut on the title-page
is in keeping with the subject of the book. The book is quite
perfect, and a fair specimen of Henry Peter's press; with the
exception of the soiled title-page, and a few of the leaves at
the beginning it is not in bad condition.

COCHLÆUS, Joannes. Commentaria de actis et scriptis
Martini Lutheri Saxonis, Chronographice ex ordine ab anno

Domini MD.XVII usque ad annum MD.XLVI inclusive. Apud
S. Victorem prope Maguntium ex officina Francisci Behem
Typographi M.D.XLIX. Folio.

A fine book both as regards printing and condition. It is *very
scarce*, in consequence of the greater number of copies being
destroyed by a fire on the printer's premises.

FABRICIUS LEODIUS, Andrew. Harmonia Confessionis

Augustanæ Doctrinæ Evangeliæ Consensum declarans. Editio
secunda, priori multo locupletior. Coloniæ apud Maternum
Cholinum M.D.LXXXVII. Folio.

A scarce book, in good condition and in the original binding.

PIGHIUS CAMPENSIS, Albert. Apologia indicti a Paulo

III. Romano Pontifice concilii adversus Lutheranæ confedera-
tionis rationes plerasque quibus eidem detrahunt, etc. Coloniæ,
Anno M.D.XXXVII, mense Octobris. Folio.

The printer's device on the title-page, an heron entwined by an eel,
with the motto *Festina lente*.

With this Apologia by Pighius is bound up

ANTIDIDAGMA, seu Christiane et Catholicæ religionis

per reverendi et illustri Dominos Canonicos Metropolitanæ
ecclesiæ coloniensis propugnatio adversus librum quendam
universis Ordinibus seu Statibus Diæcesis ejusdem nuper Bonnæ
titulo Reformationis exhibitionem ac postea (mutatis quibusdam) Consultoriæ deliberationis nomini impressum, etc. Coloniæ
apud Jasparem Gennepærum ubi et prostant Anno M.D.XLIIII.

This book has on the title-page a figure of St. Peter holding two
keys in his right hand, and a shield in front of him bears a plain
Calvary cross, shewing the arms of the city of Cologne.

In the same volume is bound up

JUDICIUM deputatorum per Universitatis et secundarii Cleri

Coloniensis de doctrina et vocatione Martini Buceri ad Bonnam.

The title-page has the same printer's device as is on the title-page of Pighius above mentioned, under which the date, "Anno M.D.XLIII." This volume, besides being an admirable specimen of the typography of the time, is a very handsome volume of scarce treatises connected with the Reformation controversies.

DE ORIGINE Erroris Libri duo Heinrichi Bullingeri. Tigure in Officina Froschoviana mense Martio, Anno M.D.XXXIX. Quarto.

A good specimen of the Froschoven press, his device being on the title-page. The book is in good condition and in the original binding.

HOMILIARIUS Eckii, contra Sectas ab ipso autore denuo recognitus. Continet Homilias de Tempore, Sanctis ac Sacramentis.

This volume has an elaborate wood-engraved title-page, and many wood-engraved cuts are prefixed to the several homilies expressing the subject of which the homily treats. The date is M.D.XXXVI. The colophon states that the book was printed " Impensis Georgii Krapfii excusum Bibliopolæ Ingoldstadiensis."

In the same volume is bound another collection of Homilies, viz.,

HOMILIARII Eckiani adversus Sectas ab ipso autore denuo recogniti.

With the same engraved title-page and wood engravings of the character found in the above-mentioned volume, and of the same date; but the type is of a different kind and quality of paper and printing. Accordingly the colophon states, "Alexander Vueyssenhorn Typographus Augustanus excudebat." These two collections of Homilies form a handsome volume, in the original binding and in good condition, except that a few of the leaves in the second portion of the volume are slightly wormed.

ELUCIDATORUM ecclesiasticum ad officium ecclesiæ pertinentia planius exponens et quatuor Libros complectens.

Iodoco Clichtonæo Explanatore. Basiliæ apud Jo. Frobenium mense Augusti an. M.D.XVII.

The purport of this book is to explain and elucidate all the hymns, canticles, etc. used in divine service on Sundays and Saints' days, and more especially to explain briefly the Prefaces, Canon, and other matters connected with the Mass. The book is in good condition, with an elaborately engraved title-page by Van Goar, an old German engraver, who was chiefly employed by the booksellers. His cuts are executed with so much spirit and in so masterly a style that his prints are much esteemed. The book is very scarce, and is a good specimen of Froben's printing.

OECONOMIA Bibliorum, sive Partitionum Theologicarum libri quinque: quibus Sacræ Scripturæ dispositio seu artificium et vis atque ratio in tabulis velut ad vivum exprimitur, etc. Authore Georgio Edero, etc. Coloniæ Agrippinæ, apud Gervvinum Calenium et heredes Johannis Quentelii anno M.D.LXVIII.

The Oeconomia is an elaborate analysis of the books of the Old and New Testaments.

To this Oeconomia is added the

PARTITIONES Catechismi Tridentini.

By the same author, and printed by the same printers, whose devices are the head of our Saviour on the title-page, and the Cross with the instruments of torture on the last leaf, with the motto "In que est salus vita et resurrectio." The book is a good specimen of early printing, both in the Italic and Roman letter, and in the original binding.

SECTARUM, Errorum, Hallutinationum et Schismatum, ab origine ferme Christianæ ecclesiæ, ad hæc usque nostra tempora concisioris Anacephalæoseos. Una cum aliquantis Pigardicarum Wiglesticarum et Lutheranarum hæresum confutationibus Librorum partes tres, quarum prima in libros partiales secernitur octo. Francophordie ad Oderam anno M.D.XXVIII.

This book has no printer's name, and is in all probability among the earliest of the few books that were printed at Frankfort-on-the-Oder. The compiler of the book was Conrad Wimpian, a great opponent of Luther, and was at the head of the university founded at Frankfort-on-the-Oder in 1506. To each of the three parts into which the work is divided there is a highly ornamented title-page, each different from the others in many particulars, and all affording good specimens of the art of wood engraving. The contents of the book afford an elaborate list of the errors with which Wickliff, the Hussites, Lutherans and other opponents of the Church of Rome were charged by the Romanists. The book is slightly wormed, especially as regards the first few of the leaves, in other respects it is in sound condition. Initial letters are in wood engravings, some of them large.

DEFENSIO Regie assertionis contra Babylonicam Captivitatem per Reverendum patrem D.D. Johannem Roffensem Episcopum. In quæ respondet pro illustrissimo eodemque doctissimo Henrico VIII. fidei defensore ad maledicentissimum Martini Lutheri libellum in eundem Regem scriptum plusquum impudentissime. Colonie in officina honesti civis Petri Quentel, Anno M.D.XXV, mense Julio.

The book is in 12mo, having the royal arms of Henry VIII. engraved on the title-page.

AIMOINI Monachi, inclyti Cœnobii, D. Germani a Pratis, Libri quinque de Gestis Francorum. Ejusdem Aimoini libri duo de inventione et translatione corporis S. Vincentii Levitæ et Martyris, numquam antea impressi. Abbonis discipuli Aimoni libri duo de obsessa a Nortmannis Lutecia. Chronicon Casinense Leonis Marsicani Cardinalis et Sanctæ Apostolicæ sedis Bibliothecarii. Inventio SS. corporum Placidi Abbatis, ac sociorum ejus martyrum. Libri miraculorum B. Mauri Levitæ et Abbatis hactenus prælo typographico ignotus. Benedictina, a Benedicti Papa XII. nomen sortita. Et alia plura quæ post indicem capitum Aimoini recensita offendes. Omni autem studio et opera Fratris Jacobi du Breul Monachi S. Germani a Pratis. Paris, printed by Ambrose and Jerome Drovart; sub scuto Solari via Jacobæa, 1603.

A fine copy and a splendid specimen of printing.

OMNIA quotquot extant D. Ambrosii Episcopi Mediolanensis Opera.

Five vols. bound in three. An amended reprint of the edition revised by Coster. Printed at Basle by Eusebius and Nicholas Episcopius, M.D LXVII. The title-page bears Episcopius' (the father) well-known device. The book is a good specimen of printing, with a good broad margin.

BEATI Joannis Damasceni opera omnia. Item: Joannis Cassiani Eremitæ non prorsus Dissimilis, etc. Accessit, Joannis Damasceni operibus, itemque Cassiani, etc.; Index. Basilia ex officina Henrici Petri, 1575.

This volume contains some good specimens of Greek type.

HEMMINGIUS, Nicholas, Commentaria in Evangelium secundum Johannem, Pars Prior. Basileæ per Conradum Waldkirch, 1591.

The title-page of the first part is an elaborate wood-engraving, and both parts have the printer's device.

Bound with this Commentary is

COMMENTARII in Evangelium secundum Matthæum, Marcum, Lucam, ex ecclesiasticis Scriptoribus collecti, Novæ Glossæ Ordinariæ specimen donec meliora Dominus.

Then occurs the device (an olive tree) of Robert Stephen, and at the foot of the title-page, "Oliva Roberti Stephani M.D.LIII." An excellent specimen of that eminent printer's work.

POLYDORI Vergilii Urbinatis Anglicæ Historiæ Libri viginti sex. Ab ipso autore postremum jam recogniti adque amussim salva tamen historiæ veritate expoliti. Edited by Simon Grynæus. Basiliæ apud Mich. Isingrinium, anno M.D.XLVI.

Isingrin's device is engraved on the title-page, and the book is a good specimen of printing. Folio.

68

GILB. GENEBRARDI Theologi Parisiensis etc. Chrono-
graphiæ libri quatuor.

Printed at Paris "apud Michaelem Sonnium via Jacobæa sub
scuto Basiliensi 1580."

In the same volume is bound

CHRONOLOGIA Hebræorum.

The same author and printer and date.

ORTHODOXOGRAPHA, Theologiæ sacrosanctæ ac syn-
cerioris fidei Doctores numero LXXVI ecclesiæ.

Printed at Basle by Peter, 1555. This is the *first* and very scarce
edition. The work is edited by J. Jas. Gynum, and is usually in
two volumes. The title-page bears Peter's well-known device,
but his name does not appear. The reprints of Tatian's Oration
against the Gentiles and that of Theophilus ad Autolycum contain
good specimens of the *Greek* type of the time.

FRATRIS Baptiste Mantuani carmelite. Parthenice secunda que et Catharinaria inscribitur additis Vaurentini argu-
mentis: et annotationibus ab Ascensio familiariter exposita.
Per quem Venustum hoc opusculum nuperrime magna diligentia castigatum fuit: cui complures accesserunt adnotationes:
quibus hoc signum * prepositum candidus lector videbit.

Then follows the device of Peter Marescal of Lyons, with the date
1525; the whole title enclosed in an engraved border. At the
end of the book is a short colophon: "Impressum Lugduni per
Antonium du Ky, Anno domini 1525." Small quarto; Gothic
type. A good specimen of the printing of that date.

BUCOLICA Mantuani. With the Commentary of Andrew
Vaurentinus. The colophon is as follows: Finiunt uberrima
commentaria Andree Vaurentini Serrani in Bucolica fratris
Baptiste Mantuani Carmelite, de novo correcta et emendata
atque impressa Lugd. per Joannem Crespinum. A.D. 1526.

The book is in small quarto; Gothic type.

FRATRIS Baptiste Mantuani Carmelite: Theologi: Poete: ac Oratoris clarissimi. De contemnenda morte carmen. Eodem Coroneo Miscellaneo Paraphraste et interprete.

Then follows the device of Eustache Mareschal: "Venale prostat Elegantissunum hoc opus Tolose in edibus Eustachii Marescalli. In vico Partarietis." The book is in small quarto, Gothic type, that of the poem being large bold type, that of the paraphrase smaller. The work is without date, but probably printed soon after 1500.

PROBE uxoris Adelphi opusculum.

This professes to be the "Cento Virgilianus" of Proba, the wife of the consul Adelphus, in the time of the emperor Nero, but is more accurately regarded as the production of Falconia, the wife of a Roman noble at the time when Rome was besieged by the Goths. The verses of this lady, which describe some of the most striking events recorded in the Old and New Testament, were very popular in the Middle Ages, and were several times reprinted during the 15th century.

AUREUS de morte Libellus. The dedication begins thus: Joannes Coroneus Miscellaneus, Carnutensis, dignissimo Appamiarum Episcopo, domino Bernardo Lordato, domino a Casa Nova, Salutem plurimam dicit.

The dedication is followed by a table of the words explained in the treatise. After which the work itself follows in eighteen brief chapters, each of which is called *Tomus*. There is neither printer's name, place, nor date, but the full title of the work is given on fol. 1, thus: "Joannis Coronei miscellanei Carnutensis viri eloquentis aureus de morte libellus ex his quæ in Marcum Tullium ad historiam scripsit decerptus." The volume, which consists of 32 pages besides the dedication and table of words, is very beautifully printed in black letter about the first half of the 16th century, and concludes with some verses commendatory of the work, written by Petrus Cassanus. The work seems to be a digest of the contents of Petrus Mantuanus' "de Morte contemnenda."

DEFENSORIUM elucidativum observantie regularis fratrum

minorum: editus a reverendo P. Bonifacio provincie Francie ministro.

The book is scarce; it is in Gothic type, small quarto, with signatures, but no pagination or running title. No date or name of printer or place.

SERMONES Dominicales de tempore et de sanctis pro totum annum, eximii doctoris fratris Jacobi de voragine ordinis prædicatorum, quondam archiepiscopi Januensis, cum registro eorumdem in prī.

Below this title occurs a wood engraving of the Archbishop preaching to a congregation. The colophon states that the book was printed at Pavia by Jacobus de Paucis-drapis, 1499. It is a good specimen of that press. The volume contains only the Sermones Dominicales; it is in small clear Gothic type, double columns, 51 lines in a column, 179 leaves. On the dorso of last leaf is the register of catch-words and the printer's engraved monogram.

BERTHOLOMEUS de Proprietatibus Rerum, translated by Trevisa. Printed by Thomas Berthelet, 1535.

On the dorso of the last page is the printer's device, which is frequently wanting. The title-page, though supplied, is an exact copy of that printed by Berthelet.

ANTONII Sadeelis Viri Clarissimi Vereque Theologi de Rebus Gravissimis Controversis Disputationes accuratæ Theologice et Scholastice Tractæ. Ex officina Thomæ Thomasii Inclytæ Academiæ Cantabrigiensis Typographi. 1584.

Bound with this work is an Account of a Voyage from Antwerp to Spain, India, etc., in 1534—1554, by Hulderic Schmidel; without name of printer or place. Both books are in small quarto.

SPECULUM Animæ: seu soliloquium: Heinrici de Hassia maximi theologi secularis. Contra poetas pro theologis epistola Joannis Campani. De poetarum infælicitate carmen Fausti. In theologorum laudem versus ejusdem. Elegia

Joannis pape **xxiij** in concilio Constanciensi depositi. Elegia Sebastiani Brant: in mortem Philippi regis Castelle filij Maximiliani regis.

It is to be observed that J. Wimphelinge, who superintended the reprint of H. Langenstein de Hassia's "Speculum Anime," John Campanus, Sebastian Brand, and others, were chiefly friends and contemporaries of Erasmus. The colophon states that the book was printed at Argentoratum by John Knoblouch, 1507. This volume is small quarto, in bold Roman type, and is a good specimen of the press at that time.

SACERDOTUM defensorium. Christopheri Scheurli Juris Utriusque Doctoris libellus de Sacerdotum ac rerum ecclesiasticarum præstantia, tam Christianis quam ethnicis exemplis abunde demonstrans Deo dicatis bonis sub interminatione futuri et præsentis judicii laicis abstinendum fore atque parcendum. Clericos autem etiam malos honorandos et cum eorum bonis divino ac humano jure ab omnibus exactionibus et muneribus ita immunes esse, ut eis aut rei ecclesiasticæ injuriantes anathema sint et plerumque mala morte pereant.

The colophon states that the book was printed at Nuremberg in 1513 by Joannes Weyssenburger, Sacerdos. The book has been bound and the margins somewhat cut away, but it is otherwise in good preservation.

MARTYRILOGIUM Usuardi monachi quod ad karolum magnum scripsit. Cum additionibus olim ex diversis martyrologiis collectis, et adjectis atque jam in non paucis locis auctis. Huic autem operi premittuntur epistolæ quædam et prefationes ex quibus liquido appareat quantum deceat quantumque expediat sanctorum memoriam assidue agere. Here follow mottoes: 1st, from Gerson super Magnificat tractatu octavo; 2nd, from Leo papa in sermone epiphanie. The colophon begins: Finis martyrologium usuardi monachi, cum additionibus ex diversis martyrologiis multo sudore collectis separatimque jam secundo anno domini millesimo quingentesimo vicesimo primo apud Coloniam Agrippinam adjectis. Duodecimo.

PUPILLA oculi omnibus christigenis Sacerdotibus tam curatis quam non curatis pernecessaria : per magistrum Johannem de Burgo Cancellarium alme Universitatis Cantabrigiensis et sacre theologie professorem compilata. In qua tractatur de septem sacramentarum administratione. Item de decem preceptis decalogi. Et de reliquis ecclesiasticorum officiis que oportet sacerdotem rite institutum non ignorare. Nuper accuratissime correcta, emendata, ac mille in locis castigata atque vigilanti oculo in pristinam lucem redacta. Then follows : Herasticon ad quendam invidum. Veneunt hec Parrhisii moderato preciosa Johanne parvo Universitatis Parrhisiensis bibliopola sub intersignio II. III. In via Jacobea.

This is one of the later and more accurate editions of this once very popular clerical Vade-mecum. See Tanner, p. 431; Pitsius, p. 542.

FRATRIS Hieronymi Savonarolo Ferrariensis Ordinis Predicatorum. Triumphus crucis de fidei veritate. Post novissimam impressionem alias Venetiis excussam. Denuo nunc primum a bene docto Theologo adamussim recognitus : cunctisque mendis expurgatus. (12mo.) Colophon : Finit solemnissimum opusculum : in quatuor libris distinctum : de veritate fidei catholice : editum ab eximio theologo fratre Hieronymo savonarola : ferrariensi. Impressumque Venetiis per Alexandrum de bindonis. A.D. 1521.

On the title-page is a wood engraving representing Savonarola in his study. On the dorso of the last leaf is an engraving of the city of Venice under the figure of Justice. Above are two shields. Below are the printer's initials, A. B. The book is an excellent specimen of the Venice press; it is clean and perfect, and in the original vellum binding.

MEDITATIONES Sanctorum cum aliis piis opusculis hoc ordine digestis. In primis carmina in laudem hujus operis. Item carmina Pii pape II. in laudem beati Augustini episcopi. Item tabula capitularis super omnia opuscula hic contenta.

Meditationes sancti Augustini episcopi Hipponensis. Solilo-
quia ejusdem. Manuale ejusdem. Meditationes sancti An-
selmi Cantuariensis archiepiscopi. Meditationes sancti Bernardi abbatis. Epistola ejusdem de perfectione vite. Sermo
sancti Bernardi de passione Domini. Mirabile dictum Petri
Damiani de hora mortis. Tractatus sancti Vincentii de vita
spirituali. Item carmina Mapphei Vegii in laudem beate
Monice.

The book is in good Gothic type, but without date, name of printer
or place; in good clean condition, and in the original vellum
binding; the paging is in MS. by some former possessor of the
book.

SERMONES DECLAMATI coram alma Universitate Canta-
brigiensi per venerandum patrem fratrem Stephanum Baronis
fratrum Minorum de Observantia nuncupatorum regni Angliæ
provincialem vicarium ac confessorem regium. Diligenter impressi in Academia Parrhisiensi. In quibus imprimendis ordo
prioris impressionis non sine concilio quibusdam in locis mu-
tatus extitit.

The book is without printer's name or date, has a running title and
table of principal matters, and is perfect. See Pitsius, p. 696,
Pulton's *English Franciscans*, p. 222, and Tanner's *Bibliotheca*,
p. 77.